A Happier, Healthier And Wealthier You

Overcome Self-Sabotage and Boost Your EQ
to Thrive In Business…and Life!

Rebekah Ryan

A Happier, Healthier And Wealthier You: Overcome Self-Sabotage and Boost Your EQ to Thrive in Business… and Life!

Rebekah Ryan

ISBN: 978-1-7635892-2-3

First Printing 2024

This book was formerly published as, 'The 7 Saboteurs of Success: Stop Self-Sabotage and Boost your EQ to Thrive in Business… and Life!

Rebekah Ryan
7 Hudson St, Hamilton. N.S.W. 2303 Australia
www.rebekahryan.com
Email: rebekah@rebekahryan.com

"The happiness of your life depends upon the quality of your thoughts."

—Marcus Aurelius

What Clients Are Saying:

"I went to Rebekah after reading reviews with positive results from people being stuck! I wanted to move past the stuck feeling too. I have been working with a psychologist for five years (who I am truly grateful for and has assisted me through some really tough times) but constantly could not get past the stuck feeling. I have struggled with financial situations (with massive anxiety around money), personal relationships, social anxiety, and work.

Examples of things that were happening for me included:

- I would receive a bill and instantly would feel sick (even though I would have the money to pay this).
- The thought of making a phone call would send me in to a spin either at work or personally.
- Visiting close friends and family would cause me to be very emotional.
- I had OCD.
- I always went to the worst case scenario when things popped up: I was always negative.
- I woke everyday day tired, exhausted, and felt heavy.

"I have lived with anxiety since childhood, and today, I can honestly write that Rebekah has changed my life forever. Rebekah listened with no judgement and assisted me to shift my thought patterns…Now I wake, ready for whatever the day brings with tools that I will have with me for life. I am positive. I enjoy being with friends and family. I have a budget and do not worry about bills rolling in. I can make a phone call straight away with no ill feelings and, best of all, I am happy, present, calm, and relaxed!"—A.C.

"Wow! I cannot thank you, Rebekah, enough for all the help over the sessions we've had recently. I feel like a changed woman! Saying goodbye to being an anxious, sleep-deprived mess. You've really helped me tackle my anxiety, mistrust, and fears and also taught me how to handle situations for the future. I'll come back and update this in 12 months, but I truly feel like I've made life-lasting changes with you. Thank you!!!"—A.R.

"I think Rebekah could help you with just about anything. SHE CHANGED MY LIFE, my mindset, my attitude, and how to deal with a few things. She has helped me with a particular PTSD situation to the point where now it has no effect on my life—I can acknowledge it without any bad feelings. She has made my "big worries" become small, and I now don't sweat the small things. I can enjoy my life far more. I will be seeing Rebekah again for more personal growth opportunities that come up in my life. Thank you so much for what you have helped me with. I'm extremely grateful and so glad I took the step to work with you. I wish I had found you years ago!"—K.C.

"I went to see Rebekah after going through 18 months of extreme resentment, depression, anxiety, and overall, feeling lost and unfulfilled. I truly did not see a way out before seeing Rebekah. Six weeks working together, I am honestly blown away with the results. I now wake up feeling energetic and excitement for my life and have formed so many small new habits that are leading to a better life. I cannot recommend Rebekah enough. Her warmth and kindness make her so easy to connect with, and she is amazing at what she does."—N T.

“I've been dieting and restricting for over 20 years but never found anything I could stick to or do without it being all-consuming and stressful. After working with Rebekah, I now find making healthy lifestyle choices so easy, like second nature. My sugar cravings disappeared! Thinking about my weight and food took up so much 'mental real estate,' but now I feel free of that, and I can use my brain power for so much more. My sessions with Rebekah helped me change my mindset and shed weight, and overall, I'm so much happier. Thank you!”—J.P.

“Before working with Rebekah, I was feeling pessimistic and felt there were no answers. After the short time of working with her, I truly feel I have grown as an individual and have learnt so much about myself and life. Really helping me peel back the layers of negative thinking patterns and behaviours. Rebekah is extremely knowledgeable about the mind, and I cannot be more thankful for how she has helped me overcome adversity.”—T.L.

“My loving partner Googled Rebekah & recommended I see her for behaviours that were not serving me well. I felt angry and I did not like myself much. Rebekah has been a life changer. I felt very comfortable and trusting of Rebekah and she has helped me work through my issues.

After many tears, giggles, and a great toolbox of techniques to use in everyday life.

I feel happy and look forward to every day.”—S.P.

Taken with thanks to my clients (and very slightly edited) from my Google reviews 2024.

Dedication

This book is dedicated to:

My father, Paul (1944–2020), who instilled a love of reading and in his library kept some wonderful books, including *Psycho-Cybernetics*, that planted a seed.

My mother, Suzanne, for her love, encouragement, and a "You can do anything you put your mind to" attitude.

My gorgeous sons, Lachlan and Alexander: being your mum is the greatest blessing of my life; love you to the moon and back! Follow your dreams…

Table of Contents

Acknowledgements

I'd like to thank my clients who have taught me so much—demonstrating strength, resilience, and the capacity of the human spirit to grow and embrace joy. I have immense respect for you and delight in your success.

This book may not be here today without the guidance of Dr. Richard Nongard, founder of the www.twelveweekbook.com program. Richard is both knowledgeable and generous, making the dream of publishing a book very achievable, even if it has taken much longer than twelve weeks! Thank you, Richard, for lighting the way and creating a supportive community of writers to walk beside.

A special thank you to my editor, Ita de Groot. She has been so supportive and encouraging, giving kind, constructive feedback. Ita has a keen eye for detail and the ability to see the big picture, a winning combination for any editor, enabling her to make invaluable suggestions. Ita can be contacted via email: itadegroot@gmail.com

Thank you to my gorgeous photographer, Cleo Pedemonte. She worked her magic taking photos but the best result by far was making a new friend: www.cleopedemonte.com

Last but not least, to my family and friends. I won't list individuals… you know who you are! I love and appreciate you. Thank you.

Prologue

Human beings love stories. This universal truth applies across cultures and throughout time, whether we're sharing our stories to be witnessed, to entertain, connect with others, persuade, or educate. When someone's story touches us, and we know they feel our pain, we feel a little less alone.

"I've never told anyone this before…" is something I hear regularly.

I feel privileged to be trusted with my clients' stories. The rich tapestry of their hopes, fears, grief, joy, shame, and anger is illuminated by a new understanding. In this book, I share the stories of my clients. Although I change names and details to protect each person's privacy, often creating composites to ensure that no personal information has been disclosed, the essence remains the same.

I'd like to express my gratitude to all the clients I've worked with so far. Thank you for sharing your stories and trusting me to guide you to connect with your inner wisdom.

The recordings I've created to support you, as you read this book, can be accessed via my website: www.rebekahryan.com

This book has been written for informational purposes only and is not intended as a replacement for medical, clinical, or professional advice. Readers are advised to consult their healthcare professional regarding any treatment.

Chapter 1

What the Heart Receives, the Mind Believes

James was standing outside the boardroom and could feel the crushing weight on his chest. His palms were sweaty, and he knew he had to escape. As he made his way to the bathroom, his vision was getting blurry, and he could feel the rising panic. James would do anything to hide it from his colleagues. He'd experienced this before, but this time was different; he couldn't count himself back from the ledge and pretend it was all good. This time, he was beyond hope of regaining his composure.

James was bright. He had a shiny MBA in one hand and the drive to outperform the best in the other. On the surface, he was impressive, but James knew his real superpower lay in his ability to read other people. Unfortunately, this was cold comfort when he found himself hyperventilating and wondering if he needed an ambulance.

James had been working 14+ hour days in his corporate role, as well as pulling all-nighters when required. He realised that he was completely fatigued and needed some time off. He resigned and took a three-month sabbatical to focus on fitness, sleep, a healthy diet, cutting out alcohol, and reconnecting socially. At the end of this time, he secured a new position, but with the thought of work, his panic attacks returned.

James knew he'd addressed all the external factors and that he should be ready for the new role. However, his body told him otherwise. That's when James contacted me for support. Working together, we identified and addressed what was holding him back. We'll go into the details of his story later; rest assured that he started the new role feeling resilient, empowered, and ready to make an impact.

When you hear the word self-sabotage, what springs to mind?

Dictionary.com defines self-sabotage as "the act or habit of behaving in a way that interferes directly with one's own goals, well-being, or relationships."

When we apply this concept to ourselves, the obvious question is "Why?"

Why do we do things diametrically opposed to our goals?

Why do we fail to do the things we need to do to move the needle forward?

To be successful, and enjoy a happier, healthier and wealthier life, we need to move from just surviving to thriving. Although it's essential to examine external factors and take practical steps for well-being with regard to our health, environment, relationships, and career, I believe the most vital step is addressing what's going on with us internally on two levels—the level of thought and the level of feeling. This includes both our conscious and subconscious thoughts and beliefs and our emotional well-being.

Tuning in to our bodies and learning to process our emotions in a healthy way is essential, and this impacts our emotion quotient (EQ). Our EQ, or emotional intelligence, is comprised of our self-awareness, self-regulation, motivation, empathy, and social skills. Interestingly, research shows that our EQ is actually a stronger predictor of career success than our IQ. As Daniel Goleman, author of *Emotional Intelligence,* explains, "CEOs are hired for their intellect and business expertise—and fired for a lack of emotional intelligence."

Did you know that our bodies and minds hold on to unprocessed emotions, and our nervous systems can become stuck? Peter Levine, author of *Waking the Tiger*, observed that all other mammals complete the stress response after they experience a threatening situation. To put it simply, when a gazelle sees a tiger, the gazelle's autonomic nervous system responds to the threat of the tiger and goes into "flight"—running away. Once the gazelle reaches safety, it shakes, releasing the buildup of stress hormones and completing the stress response. This allows the gazelle to demonstrate resilience, continuing life in the jungle and responding to any future threats appropriately. In contrast, when human beings fail to complete the stress response, the emotions are stored in our bodies, and our brains can react as if we are still stuck in the original traumatic event.

Both stress and trauma are not things that happen to us; they are our responses to what happens to us. Imagine a set of identical twins, Jasmin and Jackie, working in the same office, doing the same job, the same busy day with challenging clients, a demanding boss, and rumours of impending redundancies. Now, picture knocking-off time. Jasmin breathes a sigh of relief and smiles as she walks out the door, looking forward to seeing her loving partner at home. In contrast, Jackie, who also has a loving partner to go home to, isn't moving because she's curled up in a foetal position under the desk. Same job, same circumstances, yet totally different responses. Our responses to life events are dependent upon our perceptions of the event, our previous life experiences, our conscious and subconscious beliefs, our emotional state, our attitudes, our overall well-being, our sense of agency, and our sense of support.

Working with our minds involves gaining an awareness of and exploring our beliefs and updating them, if necessary. Working with our bodies involves releasing the stuck emotions. Our beliefs are simply thoughts that have been thought repeatedly over time. Through repetition of a thought, we lay down a neural pathway in our brain. This pathway is strong and clear, and continued strengthening via repetition enables thoughts to travel at super speeds, just like travelling on a freeway. We tend not to question our beliefs. The majority of our beliefs are ingrained, and we accept them as facts. It often takes a pivotal life event for people to look within and question their beliefs; for example, facing a serious health challenge, the death of a loved one, divorce, betrayal, or job loss.

James had been facing one such moment. He'd worked so hard to get where he was, but he couldn't continue without making significant changes. James grew up in a highly dysfunctional home; his parents were constantly arguing, and he was terrified of his father. James' father was highly unpredictable. He had mood swings, was very quick to anger, and was prone to violence. James grew up constantly wary and always watching to read the energy of the room when he entered it and to try to predict his father's outbursts. James was born into this environment, and he would have even heard the yelling and been affected by his mother's stress response in utero. Even as a very young child, his heart received messages, his nervous system was dysregulated, and he started to form subconscious beliefs. Even though James would have no explicit memories from this time, his body would hold implicit memories.

What the heart receives, the mind believes—based on our understanding at the time. Our minds are meaning-making machines, always looking for similarities and patterns to file for future reference. These learnings are stored in the subconscious mind, and this frees up space in the conscious mind for our attention. For example, if you try a new food for the first time and it makes you ill, your mind will file that knowledge. At a later date, you may only need to smell the food, and then you feel an automatic aversion before you've even consciously thought, *Unfortunately, when I tried it, it hadn't been cooked properly, and that's why I was sick…* Today, it's probably perfectly safe for you to eat this food.

James grew up often feeling unsafe, unprotected, and frightened. He started to develop:

1. Beliefs about himself

2. Beliefs about other people

3. Beliefs about the world

When James' mother and father yelled at him and showed little interest in him, he started to believe that he wasn't worthy of attention. He believed that there was something wrong with him, that he was in some way unlovable. When his own parents weren't there for him physically or emotionally, he started to believe that he couldn't really trust other people and that he'd be better off just relying on himself. When James' own home wasn't safe, he believed that nowhere was really safe; the world was a dangerous place filled with people who could turn at any time.

Sometimes, we just have a feeling during an event or interaction with others. Maybe we notice something as small as the microexpression on someone's face, registering distain or experiencing a felt sensation about the atmosphere in a room. Our hearts are always paying attention. Our brains attempt to make sense of what's going on. When we're children, we have a smaller worldview and lack the ability to put ourselves in another person's shoes and view life from their perspective. If something is wrong, we tend to make it all about us. For example, imagine you're six years old and your aunt looks after you because your parents are going out and she's quite cross with you the whole evening. You might start to believe that she doesn't really like you, that there's something wrong with you, and that you're in some way, shape, or form a nuisance. At six years old, you have no way of knowing that your aunt feels irritated about caring for you because she'd rather be out with friends. You just know that you feel unwanted, and although you try really hard to please her, you get sent to bed early and you feel unloved. Your heart receives this hurt, and your mind makes up a story or a "belief" about what happened and what it means.

Some of these beliefs are easily recalled and readily available for us to examine at the conscious level, while others are stored deep within our subconscious. Our beliefs affect every decision we make. Many of these beliefs are created during childhood and affect us throughout our lifetime.

Carl Jung sums it up so powerfully… *"Until you make the unconscious conscious, it will direct your life and you will call it fate."*

The good news is that beliefs can be updated just like programs on a computer. Old beliefs can be erased and new beliefs installed, and the emotions we've held onto can be processed. As you read and implement the ideas in this book, you'll be updating your subconscious beliefs and increasing your emotional intelligence. The old, unhelpful, unnecessary beliefs will be identified, examined, and released, clearing the way for your new empowering beliefs.

Your EQ will be raised initially through increasing your self-awareness and ability to self-regulate. When this occurs, it's far easier to see a situation from a higher perspective and experience more empathy as you more readily consider other people's feelings and views. This will increase your overall sense of well-being, and from this empowered place, intrinsic motivation emerges. Social skills aren't directly addressed but will be impacted because just being able to hit the pause button between emotion and response enables us to be more socially adept because we're approaching situations from a place of inner peace.

Now it's time for some reflection…

Do you engage in self-sabotaging habits of thought, feeling, or action?

Are you building a seemingly impenetrable wall between you and the success you desire?

In this book, I will share with you how you can overcome self-sabotage, process your emotions, upgrade your thinking and harness your energy to ultimately gift yourself increased peace and positivity, tune into your purpose, and expand your impact through increased performance and profit. This can be applied to both your work life and your personal life.

In my work, I find that our conscious and subconscious beliefs affect every aspect of life, so I never confine a conversation to only one area if another life domain is impacting it. Although when we go to work, we wear one particular hat, in life, everything is connected. Our personal life can impact our work life; our work life can impact our friendships, and our friendships can impact our health. We work with what is figural—that which the client brings to the room in that moment—so approach this book with the understanding that although we might be tempted to compartmentalise our challenges, there are always connections below the surface, so you'll benefit from looking at your life holistically.

Veronica found that no matter what she did, her waistline kept expanding. She'd tried everything she could think of—diets, diet shakes, pills, gym memberships, and online support groups with eating plans. She'd even been to the doctor to explore if a medical issue was causing the problem. Nothing worked! Or it would work for a day or two, and her eating habits would improve, then it just felt too hard, and she lacked the motivation to continue.

Veronica was trapped in a cycle of bingeing daily on chocolate and takeaway food. She had an aversion to cooking or preparing any food at home. One day, at the end of her lunch break, she returned to the office, having just eaten two chocolate bars, and was halfway through a third, with a bag of sweets hidden in her handbag, when she realised that this pattern needed to change. She wrapped up the remainder of the chocolate and popped it into her bag, hoping the wrapper didn't make too much noise or draw attention to her. Then Veronica checked her emails and saw that she'd been assigned to lead a new team for the design project. She silently groaned, and before she even realised what she was doing, the rest of the chocolate was in her mouth. Strangely, she hardly tasted it.

Veronica felt the sticky residue of chocolate on her fingers and realised that she really didn't understand what was driving her behaviour. Sometimes she didn't even really enjoy the food she ate. She'd done all she could on her own, so she reached out to me, ready to change.

When I asked Veronica when the problem had started, she said it coincided with her move to a new company. She joked that they brought in too many delicious cakes for morning tea! Then Veronica said she didn't know why she was laughing. The issue was making her miserable. She felt uncomfortable in her body, in her work clothes, and this made doing presentations at work even worse. When we investigated the issue, we discovered that Veronica was running a subconscious program that it wasn't safe to be in a leadership role because she'd be getting so much attention. She didn't like people looking at her and the fact that 70% of her team were male only made matters worse. No one ever commented on her appearance, made inappropriate comments of a sexual nature, or touched her inappropriately. If something like that had happened at work, then she'd be able to understand her fear, but there was no simple explanation.

Interestingly, we discovered a subconscious belief formed when she was only twelve. Veronica had developed early and went through puberty before most of her friends. She recalled being the captain of a sports team and having to make a speech in front of the class when some of the boys sniggered behind her back and made comments because Veronica was one of the first girls to start wearing a bra. She realised that she hadn't thought about that for years but immediately saw how she formed a subconscious belief about it being unsafe to lead a team because she didn't want boys looking at her body and teasing her. This belief was causing her as an adult to want to eat to try to deflect male attention. Once we identified what the underlying issue was, we could update Veronica's program. She soon lost her desire for chocolate, takeaway food, and sweets and started listening to her body and making healthier choices… all without a diet!

I've helped hundreds of people from several different countries and various walks of life to get "unstuck," free themselves of the past, access peace, and create lasting change. During this time, I noticed commonalities and patterns that persisted despite differences in gender, age, culture, income, faith, and location. It was then that I identified seven archetypal Personas of Protection that showed up time after time. They are the personification of the beliefs, thought patterns, unprocessed emotions and behaviours that are blocking our success. These Personas of Protection will be introduced in Chapter 3, and then each persona will have a chapter dedicated to it.

If you read this book and take action, these are the results you can expect…

Results: You'll amplify the 5 Ps and experience **greater**:

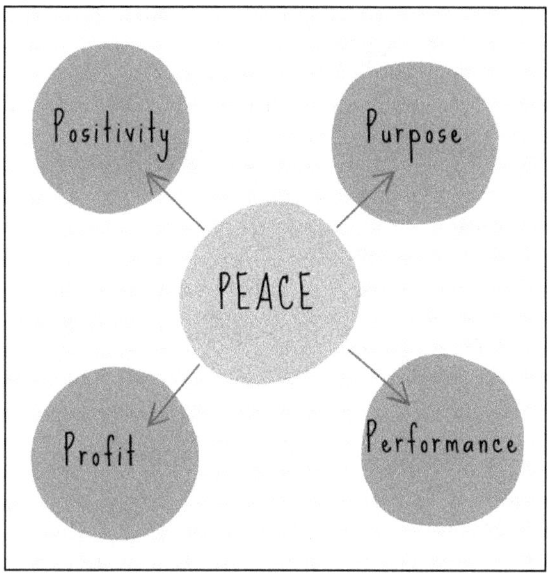

Peace – I believe that a place of peace is a place of power. It is through internal peace that we optimise our physical, mental and emotional health. Our modern lives can create an unrelenting sense of pressure that triggers our stress response and left unchecked, we can find ourselves living in a state of chronic stress. This can have serious health impacts contributing to issues such as heart disease, hypertension, diabetes, muscle aches, fatigue, depression and digestive troubles. When we feel peaceful, mentally and physically, connected to ourselves and at ease, this is when we can bring the best of ourselves to the table.

Purpose – a happy life is a meaningful life. When we can access internal peace, it frees up mental, emotional, and physical space for us to tune into our purpose. As a psychiatrist, author, and Holocaust survivor, Viktor Frankl said, "Everyone has his own specific vocation or mission in life. Therein, he cannot be replaced, nor can his life be repeated. Thus, everyone's task is as unique as his specific opportunity to implement it."

Positivity – I'm talking about maintaining a hopeful outlook whilst fully accepting "what is" right now. I'm not promoting "toxic" positivity where one has blinders on or fails to empathise with others. I'm talking about an energetic frequency that's aligned with success, and I'll be covering practical steps to give you tools to raise your energetic frequency.

Performance – the Personas of Protection whisper in our ears, distracting us and limiting our performance. To engage at peak performance and enter flow states, we need to come from a place of peace and take aligned action combined with supportive environmental set-ups. We can plan for our success.

Profit– how would you like to profit from reading this book? What does true wealth mean to you? For some people, it's an increased income; for others, it's shorter working hours and more time with loved ones; for others, it's a more nuanced, curated life with fewer things and more conscious choice and meaning. You get to choose what it means to you.

Our Personas of Protection are built on habits of thought, habits of feeling, and habits of action. It has taken time and repetition for them to become our automatic, default way of being in the world. Warren Buffet didn't become wealthy just by saving his pocket money one week. In the same way, it's what we do repeatedly over time that counts, and this book will give you the understanding and tools to overcome self-sabotage, boost your EQ and become a happier, healthier and wealthier you.

Chapter 2

Understanding the Problem

A Hollywood star, she was idolised by fans and had an abundance of male admirers. Professionally, she had unrivalled success—she was the most famous actor of her time and won critical acclaim. She was romantically linked with the then U.S. President John F. Kennedy. In 1962, Marilyn Monroe was only thirty-six when her life was tragically cut short. She appeared to have the world at her feet, yet when she passed, she had been divorced three times and was living as a virtual recluse. The coroner later ruled her death a "possible suicide."

The world asked, "Why?"

Marilyn had looks, talent, wealth, connections, and opportunity.

Why did she come to such a tragic end?

What did she fail to overcome?

She didn't overcome her Personas of Protection…the subconscious thoughts, beliefs, unprocessed emotions, and behaviours that were keeping her trapped in what must have been a bleak and lonely situation. Marilyn Monroe passed away such a long time ago. We'll never know definitively what those beliefs were. However, we can look at Marilyn's childhood and see that her mother was mentally ill and frequently hospitalised, so Marilyn spent time in an orphanage and had twelve sets of foster parents. This must have been devastating for her as a little girl and would have affected her sense of security and possibly her attachment style, sense of self-worth, and beliefs about the world.

So many of our subconscious programs, our beliefs about ourselves, our self-concept, our beliefs about other people, and the way the world works are established in the first seven years of life. In our first two years of life, we function primarily in the delta brainwave state and then up until the age of six in theta. When we're in this state of awareness, we're highly suggestible, and our parents' and caregivers' beliefs and behaviours are downloaded into our subconscious minds. Dr Bruce Lipton, author of *The Biology of Belief*, writes that this is nature's way of facilitating this "information-intense process of enculturation," because environments and social mores change too quickly to effectively pass this information on genetically. Our early experiences lay the foundation for many of our subconscious beliefs.

Do we believe that we are loveable?

Do we believe that we are capable?

Do we believe that other people are predominantly good?

Do we believe that the world is a safe place?

"Give me the child until he is seven, and I will show you the man."
—Aristotle

Although they can be formed at any stage of life, many of the subconscious programs for our thoughts, beliefs, and behaviours are established in childhood. Even though they may have been there for many years, they don't need to be permanent. These programs can be updated, and new programs established throughout our lives. We witness this when we see other people successfully creating change.

Yet just knowing that change is possible often isn't enough.

Even when you know that there's a potential solution to your problem because you've seen or heard of other people overcoming similar challenges, you relate to their stories and hold them up as undisputable evidence that change is possible. Sometimes, this is not enough.

Even when you know that it's something internal that's holding you back, this knowledge alone is not enough.

Even if you're connected with your big "Why" and there's cause for motivation… sometimes, even this is not enough. Sadly, most of us know amongst our families and friends of people who had a health condition, a family who loved them, and a doctor's orders to stop smoking or lose weight, and yet this still wasn't enough.

You may now be asking; "What is enough?"

We need to do the inner work to overcome staying "STUCK."

S: Subconscious mind and Personas of Protection need understanding & stagnant emotions need releasing.

T: Thoughts, beliefs, and behaviours: Identify what's not serving you.

U: Unconditional positive regard: Apply this to yourself.

C: Consequences of your thoughts, beliefs, and behaviours: Identify all the layers.

K: Knit together the new thoughts, beliefs, and behaviours.

When we feel stuck, sometimes it feels easier to look for solutions outside ourselves, but that rarely works. It's much like going out at night, losing your car keys, and only looking under the streetlight. You're not going to find them there if they were dropped on the opposite side of the road! It's essential to look in the right place.

S: Your subconscious mind and Personas of Protection need understanding & stagnant emotions need releasing.

Now let's get clear on the difference between your conscious and subconscious mind. Your conscious mind is responsible for logical thinking and planning, critical thinking, short-term memory, and willpower. Your subconscious mind is responsible for your involuntary bodily functions, long-term memory, emotions and feelings, creativity, beliefs and habits, values, spiritual connection, self-image, and intuition.

Your subconscious mind doesn't evaluate anything; it just accepts it, much like a storeman at a warehouse making room for a delivery authorised by the CEO. In case you didn't realise it, you, as an adult, are the CEO and have the final say over what to accept, keep, and update.

Your subconscious mind is running the show most of the time. Sigmund Freud first used the analogy of your conscious mind being like what we see of an iceberg floating on the surface while the subconscious remains hidden below the water.

Researchers disagree about the exact percentages, but the general consensus is the conscious mind accounts for between 5% and 10% of our mind. Most of our thoughts and actions are habitual. Most of us brush our teeth every day, starting in the same place, put our pants on the same leg first, and even drive on autopilot, sometimes surprising ourselves when we've arrived at our destination and don't recall the journey. We wouldn't be able to function in life if we had to consciously exert our limited brain power to give complete focus to everything we do. When we first learned to tie our shoelaces, this task required our full concentration, but over time, it became effortless, and we could do it while thinking about where we were going that day.

Did you know that your subconscious mind can be triggered by something before your conscious mind is even aware of it? This is because your subconscious mind processes up to 40 million bits of information per second, while your conscious mind can only process up to 40 bits of information in the same time frame. For example, I remember the first day I took my son to swimming lessons, and I felt uneasy and a bit sick inside. Although consciously, I knew it was perfectly safe and something that I wanted to do, my subconscious mind had reacted to the strong smell of chlorine. Before I'd even registered what was happening, I felt a fear response. I realised that this was because I'd had a traumatic experience as a little girl when a swimming instructor had threatened to push me to the bottom of the pool and jump on my back if I didn't swim the width of the pool without putting my feet on the bottom. As a little girl, I was terrified.

After I'd realised what was going on inside me and the origin, I was able to work through it so that the smell of chlorine no longer triggered me. Often, we'll have a subconscious reaction and not understand what's driving it.

Have you ever wanted to get out of your own way because you can see that it's your own habits of thought, feelings, or actions that are holding you back?

Hello, self-sabotage!

Self-sabotage is when we do things that block our success. For example, staying up really late on a Sunday night and sleeping through our alarm when we know we've got a huge presentation to do at 9:00 a.m. for the general manager. Or beginning a new relationship and, instead of simply enjoying it, constantly looking for signs that it's going to end, being critical, and starting arguments. Other times, we fail to do things, such as taking action when we get a brilliant business idea. We end up procrastinating, and six months later, see someone else implementing the very thing we wanted to do.

I'm in two minds about the term "self-sabotage." On the one hand, some clients who use it can be very down on themselves because they've been unable to create change by themselves, or they believe that their subconscious is deliberately working against them. Just to be clear… our mind always wants to keep us safe and runs all subconscious programs in the belief that they are helpful, protective, and essential. We don't have an internal part that's "out to get us" deliberately sabotaging our success; it's just a case of old faulty programming. This programming may have worked for us at some stage, but it's not serving us now.

On the other hand, it's an empowering term when we understand that we can take responsibility for how we move forward in a situation, the choices we make, and the beliefs we update. So that's the way I use it.

Our Personas of Protection are built on habits of thought, habits of feeling and habits of action. Many of the beliefs underpinning them are held subconsciously, concealing our inner conflicts and motivations. These personas are formed as a response to our experiences and environment and represent our 'best effort' to function in the world and solve problems, based on our current level of self-understanding. Again, our minds are always trying to keep us safe, so I refer to them as 'Personas of Protection,' because on some level that is what our minds are seeking to do.

T: Thoughts, beliefs, and behaviours: Identify what's not serving you.

Researchers assert that we have between 50,000 and 70,000 thoughts a day. The majority of these thoughts aren't new or unique; up to 95% are the same thoughts as the day before! This only serves to reinforce the validity of our thoughts and beliefs in our subconscious mind. A belief is simply a thought that we've had reinforced many times, and we no longer question it; we just accept it as absolute truth. For example, you may be vegan and have a belief that it's morally wrong to eat meat. In this case, the belief is already accepted by the mind, so when you go out for dinner and someone offers you a steak, you don't hesitate to consider the smell, the amount of protein, and how it's been cooked and then weigh up if you'd like it. No, you don't need to make a decision in the present moment with your analytical mind because you have a belief that eating meat is wrong, and so you respond automatically, "No thanks, I'm vegan."

U: Unconditional positive regard: Apply this to yourself.

"Unconditional positive regard" is a term used in therapy that refers to the therapist or counsellor accepting and valuing their client as a human being without making judgements.

When a therapist accepts and supports a client as a person, even though they may not condone all their behaviours, it helps to create a baseline of safety within the therapeutic relationship and supports the client in developing an acceptance of themselves.

Carl Rogers, author of *On Becoming a Person: A Therapist's View of Psychotherapy,* who is credited with popularising this concept in therapy, explained, "The curious paradox is that when I accept myself just as I am, then I can change."

It is so important to approach this deep inner work from a place of no judgement. When we judge ourselves harshly, our inner critic goes into overdrive, and this can lead to feelings of shame, remorse, and guilt, which, in turn, can often lead to us punishing ourselves or repeating the behaviour because we feel hopeless and it has become part of our identity.

If we can accept ourselves and love ourselves, even though we're imperfect, it makes change easier. I've lost count of the number of times I've heard Oprah quote Maya Angelou: *"When we know better, we do better."* It's a powerful phrase, and it can allow us a new perspective on the situation. It's wisdom I apply to my own life, and I hope that you can find it useful as you do this inner work.

C: Consequences of your thoughts, beliefs, and behaviours: Identify all the layers.

As you read each chapter, you'll see examples of limiting thoughts, beliefs, and behaviours and the consequences of them. Some consequences are actually providing positive reinforcement of the thoughts, beliefs, and behaviours that we want to change! For example, you've been invited out to dinner with friends but feel too anxious to go, so you make an excuse, claiming to have a headache. You tell your partner that you have a headache, and they cook dinner and snuggle up in the lounge watching a movie with you. It's a cosy night in, but it reinforces the idea that going out to dinner with friends is threatening/dangerous and makes it harder to go next time and easier to make another excuse, limiting our social interactions. Sometimes, there are many layers involved, and different parts of us want different outcomes, so we have to take a higher perspective and look at all the consequences.

K: Knit together the new thoughts, beliefs, and behaviours.

This is the final piece of the puzzle, and doing this creates lasting change. Awareness is the first step, and this is developed as we examine our thoughts, feelings and behaviours. When we shine a light on the subconscious program, we're then able to ask ourselves if it's serving our highest good. If it's truly helping us, we can choose to keep it. If it's not serving us, we can choose to change. Identifying these subconscious beliefs and releasing the stuck emotions is only the first step; the upgrade is essential, and it's in the "knitting everything together" stage that this takes place.

Change can be hard. Using this process it doesn't have to be, but it does require dedication. Too often, human beings resist making changes because they overestimate the difficulty and tell themselves that it's too much work, or it won't work anyway, or the status quo is comfortable enough. Or they rely solely on willpower and then give up at the first or second setback.

Bronnie Ware, author of *The Top Five Regrets of the Dying: A Life Transformed by the Dearly Departing*, worked as a nurse in a hospice and wrote of having deep conversations with patients before they passed. Do you know the No. 1 regret people have when they are dying? The dying most regret what they didn't do: not the mistakes they made but the adventures they didn't go on, the jobs they didn't try, and the relationships they were too scared to pursue.

Clients often come to see me when they're feeling stuck and just can't see a way towards their desired outcome. Many can't even clearly articulate what it is that they actually want; they just know that they don't want to stay stuck where they are.

The pain of lost potential hurts like no other. It's filled with regret and remorse. I know. At times, I've cried tears for my younger self for not being brave and taking the action I needed to take. I've sat, holding space for clients, as they processed the loss associated with avenues they stopped themselves from taking and, sadly, sometimes the door to that possibility closes forever.

Our potential continually expands as we move towards it, but the key is we need to be taking action. If we take no action, we're left to marinate in "If only." I've heard it said that hell is reaching old age and meeting the person you could have become.

Have you ever suspected that your success is being thwarted by programs running at a subconscious level?

If you've ever hung your head, apologising, and said, "I don't know what came over me… I don't know why I did that."

If you've ever done something and then been told, "You're just like your father."

If you've ever said something and thought, *OMG, I sound just like my mother, and I used to hate hearing her say that.*

If you really want to do something but just can't bring yourself to take action.

If you find yourself apologising for things that you know aren't your fault.

If you don't speak your mind at work, even when you know you've got something meaningful to offer.

If you'd rather make excuses for not doing something than for making mistakes.

If you find yourself raiding the fridge when you're not even hungry.

If you're a human being and you've ever had a problem that you couldn't seem to find a solution for, no matter how much time you spent mulling it over in your analytical, conscious mind…

… the chances are that there was a subconscious belief keeping you stuck.

You're not alone. We all feel stuck at times. Our subconscious programming is powerful. This may seem like an insurmountable obstacle at times, but it's not. I see our subconscious programming more as a tool like social media.

Social media can spread awareness of an issue, and there can be outpourings of love, donations, and practical assistance to help those in need. It can also be used to slander, bully, and harass. It all depends on how it's used. So much of what our subconscious minds do is essential and beneficial. Our subconscious mind runs our autonomic nervous system, tells our heart to beat, our immune system to create antibodies; in fact, it runs all our bodily systems, stores our long-term memory, and houses our emotions, creativity, intuition, beliefs, values, self-image, and protective reactions.

In contrast, our conscious mind is the more analytical part of our mind and is responsible for short-term memory, analysis, logic, and willpower.

Sometimes, our subconscious programming hurts us; standing in between us and our goals. Again, this is never deliberate or intentional. Our subconscious mind is unbiased; it just follows a program. The fact that we have programming isn't the problem. It's the quality of the programming that's the problem.

The good news is that our subconscious programs, the thoughts, beliefs, and habits that are running on autopilot behind the scenes, can be upgraded. Scientists used to believe that the human brain developed throughout childhood and that brain change rarely occurred later in life because everything had been hardwired. Now developments in neuroscience prove that the human brain can learn throughout life, creating new neural pathways. This is neuroplasticity in action. These neural pathways are made stronger through repetition as Hebb's law demonstrates that "Neurons that fire together wire together."

Through reading this book and applying these principles, you'll be able to overcome the secret Personas of Protection that have been holding you back and create the success you desire.

Chapter 3

Meet the Personas of Protection

My darling reader,

We've just outlined the cost of lost opportunities, but despair not!

In this chapter, I'm handing you the keys to the kingdom, the roadmap for utilising this book to its fullest potential so that you can unlock the infinite potential within yourself.

If you're thinking to yourself, "Will this work for me?" …

If a part of you is feeling scared… "What if I can't change? What if it's impossible?" …

… In the words of Bob Proctor, *"Faith and fear both demand you believe in something you cannot see. You choose!"*

Let that sink in. Are you going to choose faith or fear? It's not really faith if we're believing in what we can see, that's just fact. Faith is believing in what's unseen.

It's time to expand your thinking in the knowledge that when you utilise the power of your brilliant subconscious mind and get it on board, working with you to create the life you desire, anything is possible.

Fun Fact: The word "impossible" actually spells "I'm possible."

In this chapter, I'm going to introduce the seven Personas of Protection, but before I do, I'm going to invite you to download a free recording that I've created to support you as you're reading this book and implementing the activities to create change.

This recording, when used regularly, will help create more distance between yourself and your thoughts. You can access, 'The Parking Attendant,' here:

https://www.rebekahryan.com

Ultimately, you are not your thoughts; you are the thinker of your thoughts.

The activity I guide you through only takes a few minutes of your time, but the rewards are long-lasting. As human beings, it's easy to get overly invested in the stories we tell ourselves. We get stuck in our thinking, and we can't see the forest for the trees.

When we learn to truly separate ourselves from our stories, it makes it easier to see the subconscious beliefs that are running our programs.

Remember the STUCK acronym? The **T** is all about:

Thoughts, beliefs, and behaviours. Identify what's not serving you.

If we're going to identify the thoughts, beliefs, and behaviours that aren't serving us, we need to first increase our awareness of our thoughts. Creating some distance between ourselves and our thoughts helps enormously with this.

Hot Tip: Listen to the recording right now.

Did you know that scientists have discovered that our thoughts are real things? Dr Caroline Leaf, neuroscientist and author of *Switch on Your Brain*, explains that a thought is a "real physical thing made of proteins and chemicals that occupies mental real estate in the brain as a tree-like structure on our neurons, and as gravitational fields in the mind as well as the DNA of the body."

Although our thoughts are all real, they are not all accurate, correct, or true. Have you ever been mistaken about something? For example, perhaps you were certain that you'd returned a jacket you'd borrowed from your sister, only to find it crumpled at the bottom of your wardrobe behind a suitcase six months later? Or perhaps you bumped into an old friend and they weren't friendly, and you were convinced that you'd done something or they no longer liked you, only to discover later that they'd been diagnosed with a serious illness and needed time to themselves to process.

When we create more distance between us and our thoughts, it shifts our perspective and allows us more room to question them.

I've identified seven main Personas of Protection through noticing repeated patterns of thought, feeling and action. Overcoming these Personas of Protection allows us to access a place of peace. Peace may not sound sexy and alluring, but this place of peace is very powerful. It's the antithesis of turmoil. Peace provides a secure foundation, and it is from this place that we can live with a greater sense of fulfilment and purpose as we increase our positivity, performance, and profits—ultimately creating the lives we desire.

As cliqué as it sounds, every journey starts with that first step, and by following the processes in this book, change is not only possible; it's probable. After you open a cupboard and see within, you can't "unsee" the contents. In the same way, when you understand what's driving your thoughts and behaviours at a deeper level, you begin to change. You can no longer persist in blissful ignorance… if you persist, you are actually making a deliberate choice.

And that gets deeply uncomfortable! There's a term for it: "cognitive dissonance." This is defined in the *Merriam-Webster* dictionary as "**psychological conflict** resulting from simultaneously held incongruous beliefs and attitudes."

For example, you say that you value good health, yet you continue to smoke. You don't believe that smoking is a good health choice, yet you justify it by saying that everyone needs one vice… all the while struggling internally. As human beings, we all like to be consistent, and we expect this of others as well.

Let me introduce you to the seven *Personas of Protection:*

- The Pauper
- The Overthinker
- The Tyrant
- The Mouse
- The Runner
- The Inner Critic
- The Volcano

Illustrations of All Personas of Protection

The Pauper has a poor me attitude to life, feels unlucky, and believes that "nothing ever works out for me."

The Overthinker has a "busy" mind and lives inside their head, constantly going around in circles with worry and rumination.

The Tyrant seeks to control both themselves and the world around them. They are often perfectionists and don't trust others to carry out tasks to their impeccably high standards.

The Mouse is scared. Scared to dream big, scared to speak up, and scared to really be authentic and show up as themselves.

The Runner is terrified of experiencing uncomfortable feelings and copes using other distractions such as food, shopping, and alcohol.

The Inner Critic constantly criticises, compares us with other people and keeps us boxed in, trying to avoid failure.

The Volcano is emotionally volatile and erupts with either shouting or tears.

These Personas of Protection rarely show up alone. When we find ourselves sabotaging our success, most of us are operating under the influence of at least two main personas and sometimes more. Throughout each chapter, we identify the characteristics of each persona, and I use the examples of clients to illustrate their impact. Each chapter also contains strategies to use to finally change these underlying thoughts, beliefs, habits, and programs.

The strategies I suggest are interchangeable! They are tools for your toolbox and can be used at your discretion; after all, nobody knows you like you! So, even though I suggest a specific technique to help you quell the voice of the inner critic, you may find that a different technique in the book works better for you. Different strategies resonate with different people. This is why it's important to read the book all the way through, gaining an understanding of each Persona of Protection and the techniques to use. And then, in Chapters 11 and 12, I help you put it all together with a plan.

Now it's time for some self-reflection:

What's going on in your life? Where are you getting in the way of your own success?

Consider every aspect of life that's important to you: Health, relationships, finances, career, spirituality, purpose, happiness.

Is anyone else affected? For example, a partner or children? Maybe colleagues or friends?

What do you want to achieve by overcoming these self-sabotaging habits of thought, feeling and action?

How life-changing would it be?

Make a commitment to yourself now:

I, (your name) ____________ commit to reading all this book and making time to do the inner work.

Sometimes, doing the inner work feels uncomfortable. Sometimes, we'll feel a resistance to doing it. If you're resisting some of the activities, ask yourself, "What's really going on?" Tune into the feelings inside your body. What's the message?

If it's a resistance that's saying… "I've done things like this before. This is boring," I suggest you try it with fresh eyes.

If it's a resistance that's saying… "This is silly," I suggest you approach it with a sense of play and childlike curiosity—you may be surprised.

If it's a resistance that saying… "I don't feel emotionally safe to do this right now," I suggest you honour that feeling and return to it later and check in with how you feel.

Sometimes, it's preferable to work through big issues or significant trauma with a therapist. This book doesn't replace a therapist, but it does open the door to uncovering the underlying sabotaging mechanisms and creating change. You have innate wisdom within; trust yourself.

Everything in this book works together. You can think of it as a tantalising smorgasbord. I've kept it short to make it an easy read, so again, read all of it and then choose what appeals to you. Approach it with a sense of expectancy and hope. Remember that most of our expectations, good and bad, tend to be realised.

Richard Wiseman, psychology professor and author of *The Luck Factor*, studied the relationship between positive expectations and luck and found that people who expected to be lucky experienced more good fortune than others. Conversely, people who believed themselves to be unlucky and expected negative things to unfold experienced less good fortune. He also found that luck could be cultivated by adopting the traits of lucky people. People who are lucky maintain a flexible outlook and leap at opportunities, listen to their intuition, are optimistic and resilient. If and when things don't go their way, they bounce back, maintaining hope and high expectations for the future.

How might your life change if you started to believe that you were lucky?

I'll leave you with the words of Barbara Kingsolver:

"The very least you can do in your life is figure out what you hope for. And the most you can do is live inside that hope. Not admire it from a distance but live right in it, under its roof."

Chapter 4

The Pauper

Have you met the Pauper?

The Pauper believes in Murphy's law… if it can go wrong, it will go wrong at the worst possible time. The Pauper sees themselves as unlucky, talks about others getting all the good breaks, and usually has a chip on their shoulder even if they're oblivious to it. They often have a "woe is me" attitude towards life and spend more time telling you how it's impossible to get ahead rather than thinking of solutions. They are a glass-half-empty kind of person who argue that their pessimism is actually a case of "just being realistic."

When Tim came to see me, he was really struggling and described himself as feeling, "in a rut." He had a full-time job and plenty of experience but was always passed over when it came to promotions into management. He lived with his girlfriend but was reluctant to make a deeper commitment of marriage or having children, even though they'd been discussing this for the past two years.

Growing up, Tim was the middle child with an older brother and younger sister. His older brother followed in their father's footsteps, being very outgoing and excelling at sport. In contrast, Tim was small for his age, not particularly well coordinated, and wore glasses. Tim was bullied mercilessly by his brother, but his older brother could do no wrong in his parents' eyes.

Tim's father even told him to "toughen up." He overheard his father saying to his mother, "If Tim can't even stand some rough and tumble play with his own brother, how is he ever going to make it in the real world?"

Tim's younger sister shared her mother's love of ballet and was academically gifted. She could out-read and out-spell Tim when she was only six and he was nine.

Tim felt like the black sheep.

When we uncovered the subconscious beliefs that were shaping Tim's perspective of life, it wasn't surprising to learn that Tim felt, "not good enough, not strong enough, not smart enough, not funny enough," and that he felt he didn't really belong. He didn't feel as though he fit in with his family. He felt unimportant, unsupported, and that his needs didn't really matter. Tim felt like he'd missed out his whole life and the world was a very unfair place.

It's understandable why Tim formed these beliefs. Any young child in those circumstances would form the same or very similar beliefs, so the initial formation of these subconscious beliefs was certainly not Tim's fault. However, for all of us, although our subconscious beliefs may not have been installed by us and aren't our "fault," they are our responsibility, and as adults, we have the choice to do the inner work and change.

Our minds are designed to pay more attention to anything that hurts us or is potentially harmful than to anything that's good. This is known as the "negativity bias" and is thought to have evolved from our caveman days as a survival strategy. Every time Tim was bullied or felt not enough, he would pay attention to this event, and the beliefs were reinforced.

Compounding the effect of this is the mind leaning towards "confirmation bias." Once you have a belief, you continually look for evidence to support this belief and tend to ignore evidence that refutes it. For example, if you have a belief that all men cheat, you pay lots of attention to any stories you hear about relationships ending due to male infidelity and little or no attention to the evidence of women in happy, healthy relationships with men they trust.

This happens because our brains have a filtering system, known as the "reticular activating system." It's similar to Netflix saying, "Since you watched these horror movies, we'll recommend more horror movies."

Years ago, I went shopping for a new car, took several different makes and models out for a test drive, and eventually chose a blue Kia Cerato. A week before my test drive, I didn't even know they existed. As soon as I bought the car, everywhere I went, I saw little blue Kia Ceratos. Did Kia bring in a new shipment of blue Ceratos? I doubt it! Through concentrating on Kia Ceratos, I'd programmed my mind to believe that they were important to me, so that's what my filter picked up on. Have you noticed this in your own life?

The good news is, as an adult, you get to choose the filter. After Tim released his unhelpful childhood beliefs, he could shine his attention on the present. Tim felt empowered to take responsibility for his life now and make decisions about the future.

Albert Einstein said that the most important question that human beings need to ask themselves is if they believe that they live in a benevolent universe. Whether we use the term God, Higher Power, Allah, the Universe, Source, the Divine, it's an important question to ask ourselves.

Do you believe that there exists a higher power who loves you and is here to support you?

If the answer is yes, then it makes it easier to take the perspective that *life is happening for us.*

Life often has a way of working out, even if it takes time for us to see this and our perception of life has a lot to do with our beliefs.

When we look at our lives through the lens that everything is happening *for* us rather than everything is happening *to* us, it enables us to feel more empowered. This doesn't negate the fact that there are natural disasters, illnesses, injustices, accidents, and crimes that hurt people. It doesn't automatically make everything okay. It allows us to accept what is, process our feelings, and then float higher to glimpse that broader perspective. Is there any good that's come from the situation? Sometimes, it takes time, but the sooner we can do it, the sooner we can move forward.

An example from my life was when I was twenty-three and travelling with two friends across North America with a plan to have our last stop in New York and then settle for a working holiday in London. It turned out that my friends loved New York so much, they decided to stay and find jobs. My dream was going to London, so we parted ways, and I travelled by myself. This was in the mid '90s, so no internet and no mobile phones, and I used to send postcards to my family at home. At the time, it was scary, and I certainly had some lonely moments. I was also disappointed because I'd imagined doing this with my friends. However, looking at it from another perspective, I developed resilience. I was forced to find somewhere to stay and then work on my own. I was safe. Even with my poorly developed sense of direction and the help of the *London A-Z*, I found my way around. I learned that I was capable of doing things independently. This became a resource I could draw on later on and coach myself, saying, "Rebekah, you've done harder things than this… you went to a new country knowing no one, and you were fine."

Side note: My friends didn't have green cards and couldn't easily find work in New York, so we were reunited when they came to London a few weeks later. I've never been happier to see anyone, but that doesn't detract from what I learned!

How can you apply this to your life? I invite you to try the journaling activity now.

Journaling Activity:

Take a challenging chapter or event from your life and try this. Align yourself with the perspective that you are loved and everything in life is happening for you…

Taking the "bad" thing that happened, what good has occurred as a result? What strengths have you developed? Who's crossed your path that you may never have met otherwise? Has a new pathway in life opened as a result?

If you'd like to reprogram your filter (alias reticular activating system) to develop a more positive outlook on life, the easiest way to do this is by practising gratitude.

"Gratitude is not only the greatest of virtues,
but the parent of all others."
—Cicero

Robert Emmons and Michael McCullough, editors of *The Psychology of Gratitude*, define gratitude as a two-step process:

1) "Recognizing that one has obtained a positive outcome" and

2) "Recognizing that there is an external source for this positive outcome."

Researchers have been studying the outcomes of practising gratitude since the 1950s. The science shows that practising gratitude leads to increased positivity and happiness. Other findings include increased life satisfaction and a decrease in the risk of suffering burnout (Ackerman, 2017; Sansone, R. A. & Sansone, L. A., 2010).

There are benefits both at work and in social relationships. In the workplace, if gratitude is expressed, it leads to increased job satisfaction, helpfulness, and improved productivity. In relationships, expressing gratitude helps us to "find, remind, and bind" valuing positive traits such as kindness which guide us to recognise good relationship candidates, reminds us of our partner's or friends' good characteristics, and binds them to us because they feel appreciated and are more likely to continue that behaviour.

There are many ways to practise gratitude. You may choose to write down what you're thankful for in a gratitude journal, perhaps three or five things every day. You may like to spend a minute or two making a mental list before you go to sleep. You may have a conservation at dinner time, expressing what you're thankful for that day. The benefit of keeping a gratitude journal is that you can look back over time and recall the beautiful sentiments, and the emotions will come flooding back. If you have a family, it can be fun to individually write down one thing each week and place it in a jar and then open the jar and read them all on New Year's Eve.

If you include it in your daily routine, it will become a natural part of daily life. To make this even easier, link it to an established habit. This is known as habit stacking, so you're embedding the new behaviour into an existing routine. For example, you might have a routine of walking every day, and you might spend a couple of minutes practising gratitude on your walk. Or if you read before bed each night, put your journal on your bedside table, and journal just before you read, then you learn to associate bedtime with reading and journaling.

Practising gratitude isn't just a cognitive process; it's something you feel. Really tuning into your body and focusing your attention on your feelings is the most important aspect of the practise. It helps me to take a couple of slow breaths, close my eyes, and focus on my heart, and really feel the sensation. I know I've hit the mark when I realise that I'm actually smiling… not deliberately; my smile just voluntarily erupts.

Sometimes clients tell me that they're writing the same thing every day. Grace told me that every day she'd write that she was thankful to have a healthy toddler and husband, thankful that they were building a new home, and thankful that she had a job she really loved. I suggested that the best way around this was to get really specific. For example, what's one thing that happened that day with her two-year-old son? Did he try to say a new word and pronounce it a funny way? Did he giggle playing with bubbles in the bath? Did her husband cook a fabulous dinner? Was the sunset beautiful? Was that the creamiest hot chocolate she'd ever had? How good does it feel being able to hear music?

Don't be deceived by the simplicity of this strategy! It works.

I regularly work with small business owners and entrepreneurs. They often talk about starting their businesses filled with energy and enthusiasm but feeling completely drained after twelve months. Often, they're wearing several different hats and trying to do everything by themselves, from design to accounts to marketing to sales to delivering the product or service. Even typing this feels like hard work! Workload, prioritising, and time management certainly contribute to the problem, and sometimes these issues have very logical, practical solutions. At other times, we need to look at the inner beliefs which are keeping them stuck.

Anna came to me feeling overwhelmed. She had a husband and three children between the ages of six and eleven. They were all at school now, but still, she always felt pushed for time to work during school hours, run the kids around, and do the bulk of the cleaning and organising at home. Anna's husband worked full time and his income provided for all their basic needs and the money Anna made in her business covered activities for the children, gifts, social outings, and incidental extras. Anna always felt like there was only "just enough" and no matter what she did, she couldn't seem to break past a certain income level. She couldn't afford to outsource any tasks, and she didn't feel as if she could work any harder than she already was. When Anna compared herself with other women running similar businesses and making six figures, she couldn't understand what she was doing wrong.

When the conversation turned to money, I could sense that we were heading in the right direction. Although Anna loved working with clients and helping people, she felt uncomfortable with charging for her services. When she first started, she'd offered all her work for free, and then she started charging but regularly discounted her rates. Eventually, her husband had suggested that she get an alternative part-time job and just do the business as a hobby. This led to Anna increasing her rates a little, but they were still below the market rate. Anna decided it was time to work on her money mindset.

We all have beliefs about money, and many of our money beliefs were formed when we were children. We are subconsciously guided by them unless we actively choose to upgrade them. When we examined what was holding Anna back, she recalled several childhood events that she hadn't thought about for years.

Anna had won a scholarship to a private school, and although the other students were nice enough, and she didn't ever recall being bullied, she also remembered never feeling as though she fit in. The other students would be picked up from school in flashy cars, go on ski trips, and holidays abroad, and Anna was embarrassed to bring people home because her house was very modest, unlike the palaces her friends lived in. Anna's mother was very critical of the other families and called them greedy and selfish. Anna started to develop a belief that if you are wealthy, then you must also be greedy and selfish.

Then Anna recalled an even earlier memory when she'd only been about seven and had travelled to visit family at Christmas. Sadly, one of her aunts had passed away, and the extended family had all brought lots of presents for her children. Anna saw her cousins being given lots of gifts while she got none. Of course, even as a seven-year-old, she understood that the adults were trying to help her cousins feel better, but a part of her started to believe that she didn't deserve nice things; other people needed them more. In yet another memory, Anna recalled her mother being so ill she was unable to work for months on end. This put her family in a very tenuous financial position, and Anna remembered lying awake in bed at night worrying about how they would buy food. Anna's parents ensured that she was always fed, but she remembered a feeling that there was only just enough, no extras, and never anything special or luxurious. She started to believe that only just "getting by" was normal and the way she would always live.

When Anna understood the subconscious beliefs driving her behaviour, she was able to release them. We flipped her script that "all wealthy people are greedy" by questioning it. Anna found evidence of wealthy individuals doing wonderful philanthropic work. She allowed herself to think about what she would do with a higher income, and this included living more comfortably and giving to others in need. Anna felt more comfortable about increasing her prices and earning more in fewer hours.

If you'd like to start exploring your subconscious beliefs about money, try this stream of consciousness writing activity. If this is new for you, a stream of consciousness writing activity just involves using the prompt and writing the first thing that comes to mind. Spend at least ten minutes doing this and longer if you wish. Write all your thoughts about the topic without censoring yourself. This is solely for your eyes only! Don't reread what you've written until the end. Often, after we get our immediate conscious thoughts onto the page, the subconscious thoughts lying below will start to bubble up. That's why it's beneficial to allow yourself the luxury of unrestricted time.

Stream of Consciousness Writing Activity:

Prompts:

Wealthy people are______________________________

Money is_____________________________________

In my family, we_______________________________
(habits/beliefs about money)

If you're feeling stressed about your financial situation, try on the belief one of my favourite money mindset mentors, Denise Duffield-Thomas, shares in her book *Chill and Prosper*: "There's always more money." Say it aloud or in your own mind a few times. How does it feel? When I say it, I immediately feel my body relax. Of course, there's always more money!

When our bodies relax, our minds relax, the stress hormones are switched off, and we engage the parasympathetic nervous system. When this happens, our prefrontal cortex is steering the ship rather than our "anxious" amygdala, and we can be more creative with our thoughts, and this can lead to us recognising more financial opportunities.

In my office and at home, I have a wall hanging that says,

"Today, good things are going to happen."

The more you look for the good in life, the more good you'll see. Just like little blue Ceratos, "What you focus on expands!" This, in turn, raises your energetic vibration. Like attracts like. The more you do this, the more serendipitous events fall into place. Other people feel your light and vibrant energy and respond positively. You become one of those people who happens to be in the right place at the right time… try it and see.

Marcus Aurelius, Roman emperor (161–180) and stoic philosopher wrote, *"The happiness of your life depends on the quality of your thoughts."* Let this sink in. I believe this ancient wisdom applies equally to our busy modern lifestyles.

Mantras:

I love the world and the world loves me.

Wonderful things are happening now.

Today is full of unexpected blessings.

I am safe. I am supported. I am infinitely loved.

Chapter 5

The Overthinker

Have you met the Overthinker?

Their mind is full; busy trying to untangle endless looping thoughts… one thought sparks a negative spiral. They live primarily in their head and detach from their body. They often feel overwhelmed. The only time they really focus on their body is when it's sending warning signals such as a faster heat rate, a tight chest, or a nauseous tummy. They often have gut problems. They doesn't trust themselves. Logically, they know that everyone possesses intuition but they find it really hard to discern the voice of her intuition and the voice of fear.

Miranda's main Persona of Protection was the Overthinker. It was the part of her that was positioned firmly in the driver's seat. Interestingly, Miranda's Overthinker wasn't so prevalent in the workplace. I found this to be unusual because, often, this archetype shows up in every area of life.

Although she had a high-pressure career as a paramedic, when Miranda was at work, she trusted that she knew her role. She knew she was good at it, and she just rolled up her sleeves and got on with the job. Miranda had worked with the same colleagues for years; she trusted them to support her, and because she had a very chatty partner, she just let him do most of the talking. Work was a brilliant distraction from her personal life; that's where her Overthinker reigned supreme.

Miranda's Overthinker caused her to constantly second-guess herself in almost all her personal interactions. She didn't take the lead in catching up with friends because she doubted that they really wanted to see her. When she went out for dinner with friends, she'd come home and lie in bed replaying all the conversations and wondering if she'd offended someone, terrified that something she'd said would be taken the wrong way. She'd have endless conversations with her husband, asking, "Do you think this sounded alright? Do you think they'll be offended?" She found that when he reassured her, she only felt better temporarily… then the loop would start again.

This pattern even happened with Miranda's family. Although she loved them all dearly and explained that she had wonderful parents and a close relationship with her twin brother, there was often tension with her older sister. Miranda had grown up idolising her big sister, and although they had been close when Miranda was growing up, Miranda felt a barrier between them as adults.

Miranda had been finding it harder and harder to function and get through daily life. Even though work was her sanctuary, she found herself having panic attacks at random times, even when she hadn't been aware of any worrying thoughts just prior to the onset. Her chest would get tight, and she'd find it hard to breathe. The last straw for Miranda was when she travelled to visit her sister, and her sister snapped at her for no apparent reason. Miranda started shaking, went into a panic attack, started hyperventilating, and then couldn't stop crying.

Miranda knew she had to find a solution.

Miranda had already tried some counselling sessions and medication prescribed by her doctor, and although both had helped minimise the symptoms for a few months, they didn't seem to be helping much.

Working together, we got to the root cause of Miranda's anxiety, insecurities, and self-doubt. When Miranda was in her teens, there was a critical incident that changed her beliefs about herself.

In therapy, there's a concept of Big T trauma and Little t trauma. Big T trauma is what we often associate with trauma, for example, a kidnapping, a plane crash, the death of a parent, a natural disaster, or bullying over an extended period of time. Little t trauma can include non-life-threatening events such as struggling socially at school, the loss of a pet, a relationship breakdown, or financial hardship. The important thing to remember with trauma is that the event or events themselves aren't the important thing; what's important is the way the person is affected: the emotions the body has held onto, the memories that haven't been processed, and the beliefs that the person formed about themselves, other people, and the world. *Trauma is the result of the event, not the actual event.*

How do we know if an event hasn't been emotionally processed?

We feel it in our bodies.

We think of the event or experience external stimuli, such as a smell or a sound triggers our bodies to react, before we've even registered a thought. We have a visceral response. We might feel it in our gut, or perhaps our hearts start racing. We may have an emotional response that is out of proportion to the current circumstances. Our amygdala is activated, and it all feels very real and very now, even if it occurred decades ago. This can elicit the fight/fight/freeze, or fawn response.

Bessel van der Kolk, author of *The Body Keeps the Score,* conducted studies at Harvard Medical School using brain imaging technology to explore the neuroscience of what occurs when people experience flashbacks, finding that "when traumatized people are presented with images, sounds, or thoughts related to that particular experience, the amygdala reacts with alarm… even… years after an event… When something reminds traumatized people of the past, their right brain reacts as if the traumatic event were happening in the present…"

They have an emotional response such as anger, shame, or fear and lack awareness of why they're responding the way they are to what may be a minor event in the present. We have all experienced some degree of trauma. Trauma is not what happens to us; it's our response to what happens to us.

In contrast, when the event has been processed, we can recall that it happened, but we don't get the same physical response. Our bodies feel more neutral, and we can think about it and talk about it without becoming extremely emotional. Another telling sign is that if we are reminded of it, we can register it and then let it go. Our minds don't feel compelled to continue thinking about it and replaying the event because we know that we're no longer in danger; it's behind us.

Even if "trauma" doesn't appear to be anything major to an outsider, there is nothing to be gained from comparing trauma. The important thing to acknowledge is the impact that it had on the person involved and to support them in taking the necessary steps to process it.

To an outsider, the incident that changed Miranda may not even register as traumatic. Miranda's older cousin, Eden, was home from university, and they were having an extended family celebration for Christmas. There was lots of banter around the table, and Miranda joined in teasing her favourite cousin. Eden immediately shot her down in flames, and Miranda felt humiliated. She could feel herself blushing, and then her cousin got up and left the table in a huff.

Miranda's father rebuked her. "What did you have to say that for? We were all having a good time, and now you've ruined it. We hardly get to spend any time together with all the family now."

Miranda held back tears and escaped to her room as soon as she could. Later, when she saw Eden, she tried to apologise, but Eden refused to speak to her. This didn't change during the whole holiday period, and after that, although they'd resumed speaking, Eden was always cold.

This was an initial sensitising event. It was after this that Miranda started questioning herself and wondering if she'd inadvertently said the wrong thing and offended someone. She analysed her interactions with friends, looking for evidence of something wrong. She started to doubt herself in social situations and became quiet. It felt safer to be quiet rather than say the wrong thing. Miranda started to believe that she always said the wrong thing and people didn't really like her. If Miranda didn't get invited to a party, she saw this as evidence that she was socially awkward and not well-liked. Remember the confirmation bias we mentioned with the Pauper? That is, once you've formed a belief, your brain will look for evidence to prove that this belief is true. In Miranda's case, this means that her brain will tend to gloss over or disregard any evidence that she is liked and can have positive social interactions. For example, if she is invited to join a group, she may think, "Oh, they were just being kind" rather than thinking she was really wanted as a valued member of the group. Miranda realised that the distance she'd felt with her sister was a result of the way she'd been interpreting their interactions, questioning herself, and pulling away.

After Miranda was able to have a heart-to-heart with her sister and clear the air, she started noticing all the positive interactions between them. Miranda's inner beliefs about herself shifted. Then, she showed up with more self-trust and confidence. She stated she was enjoying her social life, her panic attacks had disappeared, and unnecessary anxiety was a thing of the past.

One of the key skills for the Overthinker to develop is self-trust, and foundational components of this are developing our sense of self-worth and learning to listen to our intuition. Our intuition can be described as "the quiet voice within" or our own inner knowing. We often feel it as a sensation in our gut or our hearts and have an awareness of the message. If we're in immediate physical danger, it sends a loud signal, and this is usually easy to read. It's the quieter, more subtle messages that the Overthinker misses because they are so much in their heads.

Sonia is another example of a client with the Overthinker as the main Persona of Protection. Sonia had a very successful career in finance with a large team to manage, and she was a solo parent. On the outside, she had her life together, and people saw her as being a leader who was very in control. She was very high-functioning, looked after herself, ate well, and practised mindfulness, Pilates, and yoga. She identified more with the term *stressed* rather than *anxious*. Sonia came to work with me because she had a problem with trichotillomania. This presented as pulling out her hair; other people may pull out their eyebrows or eyelashes.

She'd had a lot of counselling, but this was a habit she hadn't been able to break. It had started when she was about eight. She'd gone through a tubby stage and had been teased about her weight by some of the other girls in school. Sonia's subconscious mind revealed that she'd started pulling out her hair as a way to relieve the uncomfortable feelings inside her body that had resulted from being teased. At this young age, Sonia had started to feel different from the other girls because of her weight, even though, looking back, she told me that she wasn't actually very overweight; she just had a bigger build and wasn't as thin as her friends. Nonetheless, at this age, she started to believe that she was different and not quite good enough.

Once Sonia gained this insight, she had a light-bulb moment. She realised that she was no longer that self-conscious little girl struggling to fit in with her peers. She was now an adult who had close friendships with uplifting, supportive women who loved her for the person she was and would never judge her value based on her appearance. She realised that although she had some issues with low self-esteem as a child, that was no longer the case.

Although Sonia now knew the root cause of the issue, she recognised that it had also become a subconscious habit. She would pull her hair out absentmindedly and more frequently when she felt under a lot of pressure. I believe that my clients all have their own unique answers to life's problems, and part of my job is to guide them to access their inner wisdom. When Sonia was in trance, her subconscious mind created a resource to deal with her busy life and alleviate the pressure. She could call on her higher self to step in, triage the situation, and make a list of what to do in order of importance. Moving forward, if Sonia ever noticed that she'd started to pull out her hair, she told herself, "I'm no longer that child with those beliefs, so I no longer need to do this," and she used the positive resource of triaging the priorities on her to-do list. It took a little bit of time, but over the next few weeks, this behaviour stopped.

Writing Exercise:

If you're stuck in a loop of overthinking, grab a pen and paper and try this exercise:

Write down the worrying thought that keeps looping around. Perhaps it's a fear of something going wrong. Sometimes this can be like our brains screaming, "What if, what if, what if…" and our brains don't wait for an answer before screaming again, much like a frightened toddler. While at other times, it's a persistent niggling whisper.

Write down the thought.

What is this fear telling me?

All our feelings are there to give us a message.

What's the message here?

Worst-case scenario?

Write down possible plans.

If we look at the worst-case scenario and make a possible plan, it can help put our mind to rest. Then if the niggling fear starts to pop up again, we can say to ourselves… "Thanks, I've got plan B." We can go a step further and write plans C, D, and E.

What if I fail my exams?

Is this fear telling me I'm underprepared? Do I need to study more or study differently? I could repeat that subject and do it next semester. I could re-evaluate.

What if I fail and let my parents down when they've invested so much in my education?

What is this fear telling me? Am I taking this course because it's what I want to do or because it's what my parents want me to do? I could have a conversation about it and tell them how I'm feeling. Discuss what's working and what's not.

Is this really what I want to do? Is there a better alternative?

Now that you've had a brain dump, take a moment to regulate your nervous system through your breath. Inhale slowly through your nose to an internal count of three, pause, and then exhale slowly through your mouth to an internal count of six. When we make our exhales longer than our inhales, this stimulates our vagus nerve, which in turn activates the parasympathetic nervous system or our rest and digest response.

Breathe in "peace" (1, 2, 3) and exhale "release," (1, 2, 3, 4, 5, 6). Do this for a couple of minutes until you feel calmer and more clear-headed.

Bring to mind a time when you successfully overcame a challenge. How did you feel? Relieved? Elated? Confident? Congratulate yourself for being so resourceful.

Now, bring to mind a time when you experienced great success. What did you see and hear? How did you feel? Amplify those feelings.

Next, write out the best-case scenario for the current situation.

____

Now write down another two positive outcomes.

____

____

What if everything worked out brilliantly? Wouldn't that be nice? Write it down in detail. Be sure to include some sensory details and lean into that lighter, more expansive feeling.

Visualise everything going well.

Did you know that researchers have studied how often worries actually come true? They focussed on worries that were more immediate and could be measured over 30 days (LaFreniere &

Newman, 2020). For example, "I'll lose my job in the upcoming company restructure" versus "Someone in my family could one day be involved in a car accident."

What do you imagine the research says? What percentage of worries come true… 50%, 29%, 17%?

No… approximately 9% of worries come true. And from the research, even when they did come true, the outcome wasn't as bad as people predicted (LaFreniere & Newman, 2020).

To put it another way… 91% of worries are a false alarm. Yes. Read it again.

Let it sink in.

Ninety-one percent of worries are a false alarm.

One of my favourite expressions is, "Worrying is like rocking backwards and forwards in a rocking chair and expecting to get somewhere." Constructive thinking is dynamic, while thought is concrete and immovable. Thinking opens us up to possibilities; that's why writing the list of positive options after we've released the fear is so freeing. In contrast, repeatedly replaying the same negative thought is how we stay stuck and strengthen the neural pathways, reinforcing it.

An analogy I once heard Marianne Williamson, author of *A Return to Love,* use is "Worry is like praying for the worst-case scenario." When our thoughts are stuck in that negative spiral, it affects our energetic vibration, and we close ourselves off from the possibilities surrounding us. This is why completing the last part of the exercise and focusing our attention on the best-case scenario is so important.

If a to-do list is keeping you up at night, try quickly jotting down the things you need to do and telling yourself "It's all written down, so I know I won't forget."

If there's one specific problem on your mind that you're seeking a solution for, do what Isaac Newton did. Think about it before going to sleep and instruct your brilliant mind to find a solution while you're sleeping. Your subconscious mind is extremely creative and can look at situations in a new way, especially if you reassure yourself and say, "It's okay. I trust my brilliant subconscious mind to find a solution." In the words of author, Marie Forleo… "*Everything Is Figureoutable*!" She even wrote a book with this title.

When it comes to creating positive change, the Overthinker tends to overcomplicate things and often tries to change too much at once. The Overthinker urges us to come up with elaborate plans, and then one of two things often occurs: we become too overwhelmed and don't even start, or we start and can't maintain the list of things to do for more than a couple of days and then start over with a new plan.

There is so much value to be gained in small shifts. Even a 1% change in habits or actions has amazing results over time. Darren Hardy, author of *The Compound Effect,* shares an example of a plane flying from Los Angeles to Rome. If it deviates only 1% south from its flight path for twelve hours, it wouldn't even get to Europe but would end up in Tunisia, Africa. That precious 1% can make a pivotal difference.

If you want to improve your diet, how much difference would it make to include some vegetables every day as part of your lunch? Then, after that becomes part of your new normal, make another small change. Small changes add up over time!

Think about one of your current goals… What's the smallest change you could make today that would move the needle and make the biggest difference?

Mantras:

Peace and Release. Peace and Release.

I breathe in Peace. I exhale Release.

I am strong; I am capable.

I am limitless in my potential.

My past is wisdom. My present is powerful. My future is expansive.

Chapter 6

The Tyrant

Have you met the Tyrant?

The tyrant has a "take charge" aura and seeks to control everything, often working their way up to a position of authority quite early in their career or being self-employed and running the show. A person who wants "the team" to succeed but thinks that it's best done their way. "My way or the highway" would be a motto.

The tyrant is renowned for being hard-working and tends to wear their long work hours as a badge of honour. The art of delegation is just a lofty idea. The Tyrant knows that no one else could do a job as thoroughly as they could. They don't trust other team members to do their part because "We all know that people are unreliable." So the Tyrant either retains the work themselves—"I understand it, and I'm quicker"—or they micromanage it, preventing their staff from stepping up. The Tyrant sees perfectionism as a positive trait only and is oblivious to the downside.

Mark had an overactive Tyrant as his leading Persona of Protection. Mark had started a small business that had grown exponentially faster than he could keep up with. He had an online store selling fishing and diving gear and had branched out to two physical locations as well, and in his spare time, he ran diving courses. The online part of the business was running smoothly; it was the stores that were causing concern. There was plenty of foot traffic in both locations, and they were situated about three hours' drive apart.

The problem he had was with staff meeting his expectations for outstanding customer service. He frequently travelled between the two locations and employed several part-time college students so that both stores opened seven days per week. Mark had training procedures in place for onboarding new staff and an employee of the month program with a bonus to reward great work. He tried not to give his staff too much responsibility.

One day, when he logged into our online session, he was ropeable. He'd received a customer complaint in writing, and they'd also left a one star, very negative Google review, all due to poor customer service. It turned out that one of his staff had sold diving gear to a new diver and had given out incorrect information about the products. When he was in-store, Mark always handled the sales for diving gear and answered everyone's questions. He was furious that his staff had given out the wrong information and was ready to write up a formal warning. Mark had been too angry to sleep the night before, so the first thing we did was an energetic practise to process his emotions, and then we explored his subconscious beliefs.

Mark had grown up with a single mum who'd had an unfortunate history with relationships. She constantly talked about not being able to trust other people to do what they said they were going to do and men letting her down and disappointing her. Mark's mother was very hardworking, and her mantra was, "If you want something done properly, you have to do it yourself."

Mark's father had run off with a younger woman and wasn't present in his life when he was growing up.

Through working together, Mark realised the origins of his subconscious beliefs and how he had adopted his mother's mantra. On reflection, he knew that it wasn't serving him. Since he'd only given his staff basic training on the dive sales and did most of them himself, he didn't trust his staff to do it as well as him. He had an aha moment about how he could improve the training and conduct ongoing training every three months to ensure that his staff were up to speed.

He decided that instead of giving the staff member a written warning, he'd mentor them and support them in doing more diving equipment sales so that they could increase their skills. On reflection, Mark saw that the staff member was always reliable and usually did a good job, so it was most likely a knowledge deficit, not that they were an incapable, untrustworthy employee.

Mark also realised that with the number of hours he's been working and the pressure he was putting on himself by not delegating, he couldn't keep up the pace indefinitely. He would be at risk of burnout if something didn't change. He decided to have a staff meeting and address the training concerns broadly and then monitor individual staff more closely.

Mark thanked his inner Tyrant for trying to help him and contributing to his success thus far but told him that things needed to change. He was choosing to learn to be a better leader, allowing his staff to step up and freeing some of his headspace for expansion and growth.

There are three types of people in this world: those who love a surprise, those who could think of nothing worse, and those who only *say* they love surprises. This third group pretends to go with the flow but only if the surprise falls within very strict parameters of what they'd actually choose for themselves. For example, "Sure, surprise me with a dinner reservation for us as a couple at my favourite Italian restaurant, not at the new Persian restaurant with all your second cousins." Part of this desire to control is because making the decisions enables the Tyrant to feel safe in contrast to the unpredictability created when other people are in charge.

Sarah was a stay-at-home mother with three children aged nine, seven, and four. She had a strict routine: up at 5 a.m. Monday to Friday to hit the gym and home before her husband left for work, making school lunches, and cajoling her children to get them to school and preschool on time. Sarah devoted her whole life to them and her husband.

She prided herself on shopping organic and cooking most things from scratch. She was also extremely house-proud, and even though she had a cleaner in once a week for the heavier jobs, she still spent hours washing, sorting, and tidying. Sarah was very involved volunteering at the school and taking her children to extracurricular sports and activities.

When Sarah came to see me, she had trouble articulating exactly what the problem was. She knew she should be happy; she had everything she'd ever wanted. Yet she wasn't. She loved her husband and kids, her home, community, and extended family. It all looked good on paper, but day-to-day, she was struggling. Sarah didn't sleep well. She was constantly tired. She had no libido, and lately, she'd been getting teary for no particular reason. She often felt "on edge" and found herself being short with the kids and fighting with her husband. She didn't actually miss being at work. She'd had a well-paid position as an executive assistant, and although she sometimes missed the people, she didn't miss the nine-to-five and her bosses' demands. She had plenty to keep her occupied and was never bored.

She found herself waking at 4 a.m., an hour before her alarm went off, and going through her to-do list, checking everything off. Sarah worried that she wasn't doing enough to support her children. Her eldest daughter did very well academically but struggled a bit with friendships and was often in tears after school, talking about what had happened. Sarah's son was very sporty and had plenty of friends, but he struggled with reading and spelling, and the extra tutoring wasn't helping. Sarah's youngest was a dynamo, and as much as she loved him, on his preschool days, she breathed a sigh of relief. There was just so much to do all the time. Sarah had no idea how mothers who worked outside the home as well as inside managed to do it.

Sarah was convinced that her perfectionistic tendencies were a good thing. She'd always had high expectations of herself and a keen eye for detail. This had helped her in her career, but at home, she conceded that it may not always be a wonderful thing.

When the kids were playing, Sarah found it really hard to be in the moment and was often more preoccupied with how long it would take to clean up the mess or get somewhere on time. Sarah's husband questioned if they'd overscheduled the children, and although Sarah thought that he might have a point, she knew deep inside that she found it easier to cope when life was structured and free time at home often led to fights, mess, and more exhaustion for Sarah.

As we worked together, and Sarah gained an insight into her patterns, she understood that there was a subconscious program running that had been installed in childhood. She wanted to control things because she struggled to cope with uncertainty. Most human beings flourish with a baseline of security and certainty about life. Some require more than others. When Sarah was a child, her father was in the military, and they'd moved frequently. She'd attended nine different schools. Due to the frequent moves, Sarah's mother really only unpacked the basics, and more than once, Sarah had come home from school to find that her mum had given away some of her favourite toys because they would need to pack soon and Sarah's mum didn't want to cart them somewhere new.

Sarah was quite obsessive about her home. Everything had to look perfect, so she spent a lot of time and energy decorating, maintaining, and updating the look of her home.

Her father had run the family home like an army barracks, and everything he asked had to be done immediately. Sarah did everything she possibly could to not make him angry and win his approval, and trying to be the perfect child was an extension of this.

Sarah's need for control extended to her children. She wanted to see them do well. She wanted to be the perfect mother, and anytime her children struggled, she saw that as a reflection on her ability as a parent. Sarah also had a huge desire to protect them from any pain. Although she'd never been bullied, at times, she'd felt very vulnerable moving from school to school. As an only child, she had felt that no one was there to protect her or look out for her, and this contributed to an unconscious urge to be hypervigilant about protecting her children. When Sarah understood the origin of this pattern, she was able to look at her current situation and her children's lives with more clarity. She recognised the strengths and abilities that she'd developed. She was good at reading the room. She realised that she could do challenging things like start at a new school even when she didn't want to, and that had helped her adapt to temporary roles early in her career, eventually moving into a fairly senior role as executive assistant to a general manager.

Sarah had an aha moment. She figured out that in trying to protect her children from any pain and preemptively trying to solve their problems before they escalated, she'd been denying her children opportunities for growth. Sarah would have said she wanted to raise her children to be loving, resilient, independent young adults, but she was thwarting any situation that would have provided them an opportunity to develop grit.

Grit is an important quality to foster in our children and develop within ourselves. Angela Duckworth's research demonstrates that grit is a superior predictor of success, above intelligence, talent, or any other factor. In her book, *Grit: The Power of Passion and Perseverance*, she defines grit as "a combination of passion and perseverance for a long-term goal." Grit involves staying the distance, changing the route or short-term goals as necessary while keeping our focus on the long-term goal. To be gritty, we need to bounce back from rejections and view failure as feedback. Processing our emotions and then reflecting helps us to do this.

When life doesn't go to plan, it can be empowering to ask ourselves:

- What have I learnt?
- What positive can I take away from this experience?
- Even if I wouldn't have chosen it, and it's been challenging, how has it served me?
- How have I grown as a person?

As parents, it can be helpful to step back and ask ourselves these questions about our child's experience.

Sarah stopped trying so hard to control everything. She exhaled. She started to understand that life can be beautiful, complicated, and messy at the same time. Although she still loved an orderly house, and research shows that clutter contributes to feelings of overwhelm and negatively impacts our psychological well-being (Roster et al., 2016), Sarah actively lowered her expectations of having a completely immaculate home and felt better for it. She stopped trying so hard to be the perfect wife and mother and started to enjoy life more.

One of my favourite phrases is "perfectly imperfect." The Japanese have a beautiful form of art called Kintsugi, which creates new beauty from imperfection. If a piece of pottery is broken, rather than throwing it away, the pieces are put back together and joined with gold. The gold makes the piece unique.

In today's world, there is so much pressure to aim for perfection, and we often compare our reality to someone else's highlight reel on Instagram.

I made a decision to embrace the concept of perfect imperfection and apply it to myself, my family, my friends, my home, and my life. When we allow ourselves to be perfectly imperfect and accept that at times, although we do our best, our best may not be up to standard, and we all have bad hair days or make mistakes, it allows other people to be more relaxed with us. If we can recognise our shortcomings and give ourselves some grace, it makes it easier to give grace to others and for them to accept this from us. Often, the person we hold to the highest standard is ourselves, and so reminding ourselves of this truth—that we can be both perfectly imperfect and wonderful at the same time, that we can be perfectly imperfect and loveable, and that our imperfections make us unique—is important.

Do I get this right all the time? No… and that's all part of it!

The truth about control is that we have no control over other people, places, or events. Our power lies in our ability to control how we respond to life. And our capacity to respond graciously to life is governed by our beliefs and the lens through which we view the world.

If you identify as a control freak, try these activities:

If things aren't going to plan, before you react, take a mindful moment.

Just breathe… Feel your belly expand… exhale slowly. Do the technique outlined in Chapter 5, "The Overthinker," making your exhales significantly longer than the inhales. Remember, when you're doing this, you're stimulating your vagus nerve, which in turn sends a message to the amygdala to say, "I am safe."

You could spend one minute practising mindfulness. Mindfulness is all about using your five senses to bring your attention to the present moment—that powerful point in time we call… *now*.

Ask yourself:

What are five things I can see?

What are four things I can hear?

What are three things I can touch?

What are two things I can smell?

What is one thing I can taste?

Acknowledge and tune into your feelings about the situation. Process anything heavy that needs time to move through your body. Then get curious and try asking yourself… "I wonder if this could actually work out better than my original plan?" Open up to the possibilities.

Challenge: Relinquish the Reins!

Ask someone in your life to take over from you and plan something… it could be your partner organising something fun/social for the weekend… or if you have older children, allowing them to choose what's on the menu and cook dinner, or if you're the friend who always organises all the events, ask someone else to take a turn.

Every time you feel like taking over, resist, breathe, go and do something else… knowing that if you do take over, the other people in your life will have their agency removed and their capability questioned. This is especially important if you find yourself complaining that you have too much to do and not enough hours.

Mantras:

I am perfectly imperfect, and that's okay.

My imperfections make me unique.

I can be perfectly imperfect and wonderful at the same time.

I can't control people, places, or events, and that's okay. My power lies in my ability to choose the way I respond. I choose to respond with grace.

Everything in life is happening for me.

Chapter 7

The Mouse

Have you met the Mouse?

The Mouse is renowned for being timid. They have difficulty speaking up and spend their life dreaming big but playing small. Often world-class people pleasers, they avoid confrontation and put everyone else's needs above their own. They simultaneously yearn for success and fear the spotlight.

All human behaviour serves a purpose and often fulfils a deeper need. Whether it's as simple as going to bed to meet a physiological need for sleep, going to a job you dislike just to pay the bills, or going to a pottery class with friends to meet your needs for connection and to express your creativity. Everything we do, we do for a reason, even if we don't always fully understand the motives for our own behaviour.

Have you ever done something and thought, "I don't know what came over me. Why did I made that decision?"

Or, perhaps you've failed to do something, thrown away an opportunity and you can't understand why?

When this occurs, there are subconscious Personas of Protection at play! There's something deeper guiding you to make that choice, and even if it's not obvious, it's likely that a part of you feels as if you're benefitting from the behaviour. You could even be making decisions automatically and acting out of habits that have been installed at the subconscious level. Do you always automatically reach for sugar with your coffee? Or do you order the large fries out of habit because that's what you always order rather than checking in to see how hungry you actually are first?

All behaviour can also be viewed as a form of communication. When we look at the behaviour of children, it's often easy to work out what they're trying to communicate. For example, it's 8 p.m., and Molly, six, is tucked up in bed, supposedly going to sleep. She's already had a bath, brushed her teeth and listened to a bedtime story.

Now imagine that it's 8:25 p.m. Molly is nowhere near sleep. She had to go to the toilet again, have another small glass of water because she was still thirsty, and have her parents help her find her favourite teddy because he's lost in the blankets and she can't sleep without him. Now Molly's parents can look at her behaviour and see that it's unlikely that she really needed to go to the toilet, have another drink, or couldn't find her teddy by herself.

On a deeper level, Molly's behaviour communicated a need for connection with her parents. This may have been driven by a fear of the dark and a need for safety and reassurance that her parents were close by, or it may have been driven by a feeling of being left out and missing out on the action if Mum and Dad were watching television or tending to a younger sibling. We'd have to spend time with Molly to uncover the motive. As adults, when we look at an example like this, it often makes perfect sense. However, when we look at our own behaviour and what it can communicate to us, the picture isn't always as clear.

Emma came to see me feeling extremely frustrated with herself. After a successful career in the finance sector, she'd started her own business as a consultant. Although she had some initial success gaining clients, all the work from her existing network had dried up, and she found herself sitting at home, staring at the walls and talking to the cat. The small client base she had wasn't enough to keep her busy, and the idea of networking or using social media made her feel ill. She was reluctant to do paid marketing because she didn't want to eat into the nest egg she'd put away for the transition.

She knew on a logical level that her business needed to be promoted, but when it came to stepping up and taking action, she stalled. Emma found herself procrastinating. She had hundreds of excuses why today wasn't a good day: she needed a haircut, it was too far to travel, she didn't like how she looked on video, she didn't know what to say to make her business stand out when there were hundreds of other people offering the same thing…

On a few other occasions when she'd decided to force herself, something else stopped her. On one occasion, she lost her voice; another time, she had stomach cramps, and on a third occasion, she slipped over while walking down her driveway, injured her arm, and had to get an x-ray.

Emma wasn't a shy person and had experience networking in her corporate role and presenting to groups. She didn't love speaking in front of an audience, but it had always been something she could manage. Emma couldn't understand what was going on here.

We explored what was going on beneath the surface. Although Emma had felt fine networking when she was representing a large, well-known company, when she was only representing herself, she felt small and insignificant. She recalled always feeling small and insignificant in her family of origin. As the youngest of five children, she felt that her voice didn't count and she wasn't noticed. Another layer to this was that she felt uncomfortable, like she was asking people for money. Her mother had always made derogatory comments about salesmen trying to "rip people off" and "only trying to grease their own pockets." What if people at the networking event thought that she was only self-serving and potentially dishonest?

When Emma sat with her fearful feelings about promoting her business on social media, she had a recollection about being in a hostage situation and feeling totally out of control. When she recalled this event, she could feel panic in her chest and nausea in her stomach. It took a little while for her to make a connection, but then she had a light-bulb moment. She had felt totally out of control during the hostage saga, and she also felt vulnerable and not in control of what others could do on social media, whether trolling her account or taking her images and using them out of context.

After this, we uncovered another layer. Emma had been married for almost twenty years, and her husband had a role in management. They'd had very similar incomes up until now, but Emma could see that if her business was really successful, she'd end up out-earning her husband. He'd made some remarks about her that she "wore the pants" now she had her own business. This brought up another fear: that he would feel emasculated and have an affair with someone younger.

Emma had a lot of layers of subconscious beliefs to work through. No wonder she was procrastinating and ill and then having an accident. Our subconscious minds always want to keep us safe, and moving ahead with this business and doing the things she needed to do to be successful didn't feel safe at all. It felt dangerous. Once we shone a light on these subconscious beliefs, we could work through the thoughts and feelings. Awareness is the first crucial step.

Most people are aware of a possible fear of failure, but a fear of success can be very surprising. On one level, Emma was worried about appearing more financially successful than her husband and the possible effects this could have on their marriage.

Another client, Naomi, said she wanted to lose weight but then realised she'd be different from her close friends. She was already the smallest in her friendship group, and they often socialised—drinking wine and eating cheese platters—and she didn't know if she'd still fit in if she lost weight and changed some of those behaviours.

Another client, Morgan, had experienced a lot of financial success and was considering buying a new home in a very prestigious area, but she'd always lived close to her family, and she felt that they'd be saying, "Who does she think she is? Now she's moved, she thinks she's too good for us."

In actual fact, Morgan didn't think she was too good for anyone, but she did feel that she didn't have as much in common with her family and old friends.

Just play with these questions:

- What might you lose by being wildly successful?
- If you fulfilled this dream, how might others be positively impacted?
- If you fulfilled this dream, how might others be negatively impacted?

Marianne Williamson wrote a powerful poem on this topic:

Our Deepest Fear

Our deepest fear is not that we are inadequate.
Our deepest fear is that we are powerful beyond measure.
It is our light, not our darkness
That most frightens us.

We ask ourselves
Who am I to be brilliant, gorgeous, talented, fabulous?
Actually, who are you not to be?
You are a child of God.

Your playing small
Does not serve the world.
There's nothing enlightened about shrinking
So that other people won't feel insecure around you.

We are all meant to shine,
As children do.
We were born to make manifest
The glory of God that is within us.

It's not just in some of us;
It's in everyone.

And as we let our own light shine,
We unconsciously give other people permission to do the same.

As we're liberated from our own fear,
Our presence automatically liberates others.

Marianne Williamson, *Return to Love*

If you can relate to Emma and you're feeling stuck, if you see yourself procrastinating; I invite you to try this exercise:

Close your eyes and take a few slow breaths.

Tune into your body and feel the part of you that is procrastinating…

When you locate that part in your body, be still and listen…

That behaviour has a message.

What is it saying? What does it need you to know?

Thank it for the message and for bringing this awareness to your consciousness.

On some level, that part of us is usually trying to keep us safe. Our subconscious mind always wants to protect us.

Anything unknown is potentially threatening. Human beings love what is familiar because whatever is familiar is more predictable than the unknown. That which is familiar feels safe; it feels comfortable, like an old pair of slippers. It's much like watching your favourite sitcom; some of the characters' responses will be predictable and you may see some of the jokes coming, but when you sit down to watch it, you know exactly what to expect… and it delivers weeks after week.

Even if an environment isn't healthy for us, for example, an unhappy relationship or a toxic workplace, a part of us can be saying "Better the devil you know. If you leave this situation, the unknown may be even worse, so the best option is to stay put."

It's normal to feel some apprehension when we're doing something new or stretching outside our comfort zone. For example, if we're going to a job interview, competing in an event, or going on a blind date, we often don't know exactly what to expect, and we usually place some pressure on ourselves to be at our best.

Did you know that from a physiological viewpoint, fear and excitement look almost identical? We experience the same physical sensations with both emotions. As adrenaline is released and floods our systems, our hearts beat faster, and we may get butterflies in our tummies. The key difference is in the way the mind interprets the physical sensations. If we're frightened, we feel more alarmed by these sensations. When we're excited, we interpret the sensations in a more positive way and might say "I'm pumped." We could even interpret them as signs of increased energy.

We can use this knowledge to coach ourselves in situations where we're stepping outside our comfort zone. This energy flow can be used to our advantage. In fact, we can view it as essential. Imagine if you were lying on the couch at home watching Netflix… would you be relaxed? Sure. Sleepy? Maybe. Is that the optimum energetic state for peak performance if for example, you're competing in a sprint? Of course not!

Many people label these bodily sensations as stress. Kelly McGonigal, author of *The Upside of Stress: Why Stress Is Good for You, and How to Get Good at It*, asserts that "Stress happens when something you care about is at stake. It's not a sign to run away—it's a sign to step forward."

If we start to feel our heart racing, we could say to ourselves, "My body is preparing for peak performance. I can use this energy to be at my best. I'm ready." What would that be like?

Stella was a busy mum of two young children who took on way too many roles volunteering at her children's school as well as working in an office part-time. It wasn't work that lit her up, but it provided some much-needed additional income and gave her some time out of the house with other adults. When she came to see me, she was miserable but didn't quite know why. On one level, she had everything she wanted: a husband, two healthy kids, a house, and an okay job, yet she was often teary and frequently angry with her husband. When we explored what was going on, it turned out that Stella was holding on to a lot of resentment.

She appreciated her husband working full-time, but she felt that he got to work long hours pursuing his dream job while she did the majority of the parenting and had chosen work based more on how it fit with her parenting commitments than doing something she wanted to do. Stella's husband, Craig, made most of the big decisions for them singlehandedly, and Stella felt like she was just along for the ride. They'd moved for his career, and although Stella had tried to voice her concerns about moving away from family and friends, Craig had spoken over the top of her. He had a quick temper, and although he wasn't violent, his moods could be unpredictable.

This reminded Stella of the way her own mum had behaved when she was growing up. Stella's mum was highly unpredictable; funny and warm one minute and then furious the next, often yelling and sometimes cruel. Stella realised where her people-pleasing behaviours stemmed from; she could see the difficulty she had establishing boundaries and speaking up for herself. This light-bulb moment was the beginning of change.

The overwhelming desire to please and to meet with the approval of others at your own expense may be a trauma response. When faced with a threat, the autonomic nervous system switches into gear, releasing chemicals throughout our bodies. This reaction occurs subconsciously. The most commonly talked about responses to danger are the fight, flight, or freeze responses. In fight mode, we become angry and confront the threat, for example, yelling at a partner or sending an angry email at work.

In flight mode, we feel panic or anxiety and choose to run away or avoid the threat, for example, running from an attacker, walking away from a conflict with a partner, or avoiding raising a topic at work.

In freeze mode, we shut down to block out the threat. We may dissociate from our bodies and have low energy, for example, freezing in response to unwanted or overwhelming sexual touch.

Fawning is the fourth response. Pete Walker, author of *Complex PTSD: From Surviving to Thriving*, describes the fawn response as "a response to a threat by becoming more appealing to the threat," explaining that, "fawn types seek safety by merging with the wishes, needs and demands of others."

Fawning is different than coming from an empowered place and choosing to be kind or selfless. Examples of fawning can be:

- always giving in to your partner's wishes when you'd prefer not to
- apologising to people when it's not your fault
- having trouble saying no to others or establishing boundaries

If we have a history of fawning behaviour, it's important to be aware of what's motivating us. We can pause and ask ourselves, "Am I doing this only to please someone else?" "What do I really want to do?' "What aligns with my values?'

It can help to affirm to ourselves that "My needs are just as important as everyone else's. My preferences are my preferences, and I own them."

Sometimes, as children, we are rewarded for being "good" and putting the needs of others first.

One client told me that as a child, she was under enormous pressure to "keep the peace." She had an older brother who acted out a lot and a mother who had an autoimmune disease and had bouts of being very unwell, so she was often told "Just give in to your brother because if you don't, he'll keep carrying on and make life miserable for everyone." This sends a message to our subconscious minds... *Your needs aren't as important as your brother's, and you'll be praised and recognised for doing the "right" thing… being a good girl.*

Writing Activity:

Are any of these true of your childhood?

Were you stifled as a child and not allowed to pursue your heart's desires because you had to please one of your parents?

Did you have to make yourself small by being compliant because it wasn't safe to bring attention to yourself?

Did you feel as though your needs weren't important because there was too much chaos?

Were your needs neglected because everyone was too busy?

Did you have to take on adult responsibilities too young?

If so, take some time and write a letter to your younger self, acknowledge what happened, how your younger self felt, and how unfair that situation was. Tell your younger self that they deserved so much more. They deserved to be treated with love and kindness, to be safe, to be treated with respect, to be listened to and supported, to be cherished. All children deserve to be treated this way. Tell them that now you understand where the old patterns came from, you can let go of those old beliefs and behaviours. Tell this child that you've got their back and moving forward, you're choosing to validate your adult self because you're an adult now, and you can.

Mantras:

I am worthy.

I am whole.

I am enough.

I am more than enough.

My needs are important, too.

I respect myself.

I treat others with respect, and I expect this from others.

It's safe for me to be seen.

It's safe for me to be heard.

It's safe for me to shine.

Chapter 8

The Runner

Have you met the Runner?

I'm sure you'll recognise the Runner, although they're often wearing different costumes.

Your ears may prick because some Runners will frequently tell you that they have a problem with overeating or eating too much sugar/takeaways/heavily processed foods. And there are other Runners who would never admit it out loud; they eat in secret, hiding food around the house or in their cars or their desk drawers at work.

Another breed of Runner has less interest in food. Instead, they pour a glass of wine every night, and that glass gets bigger and sometimes, eventually, turns into a bottle. Other Runners max out their credit cards, spending big in shopping centres, at little boutiques, or online shopping for items they don't even unwrap. Another variety loses hours mindlessly scrolling social media or binge-watching Netflix. Although these behaviours all look different on the surface, the centres are identical.

In each case, the Runner thinks that the behaviour is the problem.

News flash! **The behaviour isn't the problem.**

The behaviour is merely a symptom of the problem.

The real problem is that the Runner bolts from uncomfortable feelings. This is understandable. It's Psychology 101. Human beings are wired to run towards pleasure and away from pain. The Runner registers an uncomfortable feeling, and as soon as possible, they seek a neurochemical fix. For example, when we eat sugar, the brain releases dopamine, the "reward" chemical. This temporarily replaces the other feelings, and we feel good. When we repeatedly go for that sugar hit, the brain develops a level of tolerance, which means we need to eat more sugar to get the same result.

Similarly, shopping releases a surge of dopamine. In fact, when we shop online, our brains release dopamine before the parcel arrives. Dopamine is released in anticipation of a reward! Researchers have found that in one study, 76% of shoppers were more excited by online than in-store purchases (Weinschenk,

2015). The researchers attributed this increased anticipation because online shoppers need to wait for the items' arrival.

Drinking alcohol also releases dopamine, which accounts for the initial feelings of well-being and confidence that people experience. However, at the same time, other chemicals are being released, which can generate feelings of depression and limit inhibition.

When we spend hours scrolling on social media, an interesting thing happens. Initially, we get a dopamine hit. This is because, as human beings, we're seeking connection, and the likes, comments, and funny videos provide this in a powerful way. Our brains want us to connect to other people to keep us safe; the old "safety in numbers" program stemming from our caveman days. The biggest problem occurs because social media use produces a huge amount of dopamine, far more than other ordinary activities like cooking or listening to music.

When social media use causes a huge increase in dopamine, our bodies try to stabilise, but instead of returning to the original base, we go lower, which creates a dopamine deficit, and we feel compelled to stay online longer, looking for the next hit.

Sasha identified the Runner as one of her main Personas of Protection. The minute she walked into my office, I immediately noticed her strong sense of style, so it was no surprise to learn that she worked in the field of fashion. Sasha had a successful career, good relationships with her young adult children, meaningful friendships, and a beautiful home. She also had a habit she wanted to break. Sasha had found herself drinking every night, even the nights when she told herself she'd have a break. A glass of wine most days with dinner became a glass before dinner, another glass while cooking, and then finishing the bottle before going to bed. She woke up feeling sluggish in the mornings, found it hard to get motivated to start her day, and felt stagnant at work. Her ideas had stopped flowing. Sasha's friends would invite her out, but she felt less and less inclined to go anywhere. She had a magazine-worthy home that many would envy, but could feel the walls closing in around her. She'd tried using willpower to break the cycle. It wasn't working.

Willpower is an interesting phenomenon. It doesn't remain static throughout the day. Roy F. Baumeister, a prominent willpower researcher and science writer, John Tierney, authors of *Willpower: Rediscovering the Greatest Human Strength*, assert that our willpower is depleted throughout the day through the course of making decisions and exercising self-control. Decision fatigue is a real thing! Every decision we need to make, even menial decisions, drains a little energy from our mental battery. So, it only stands to reason that many of us have more difficulty exerting willpower at the end of the day.

That's why many successful people wear the same type of clothes every day. For example, Steve Jobs always wore a black turtleneck and jeans, and Mark Zuckerberg always wears a grey T-shirt. It's also the reason why many successful people eat the same thing for breakfast every day and have a set morning routine.

When people decide to cut back on drinking and only drink, say, twice a week, it means that they need to make a decision every day. On a daily basis, they need to ask themselves, "Is today a day I'll choose to be alcohol-free, or is today a day I'll drink?" This is actually often much harder than choosing to stop drinking altogether. When people choose to stop altogether, drinking is no longer an option, so they don't need to make a decision about it. The decision has already been made, and they can get on with life rather than spending time contemplating it on a daily basis.

Using only willpower or white-knuckling through a change can be challenging because that battery becomes drained. When we use our subconscious mind to get to the "Why?" that's driving the behaviour and then program our subconscious mind to enjoy the changes, transformation becomes so much easier.

In Sasha's case, when we worked with her subconscious mind, it was revealed that she was drinking to mask feelings of loneliness. Initially, in our consultation, Sasha had said that she had a beautiful family and plenty of friends, and although this was true and an off-the-top-of-her-head conscious response, on a deeper level, her need for connection wasn't being met. Sasha's children were now young adults, and although there was plenty of love there, they had different priorities and spent more time with partners and friends. Several of her close friends were busier than ever with aging parents and teens still in high school, and didn't have as much time for meaningful conversation or activities. Sasha also admitted that she'd been very disappointed after dating an avoidant man and had shied away from relationships.

Working together, we were able to identify what Sasha truly valued and create a plan for success. For Sasha, changing her habits around alcohol was only one part of the picture, and this was easier knowing that alcohol was actually pushing her further away from her life goals and out of alignment with one of her highest values, which was health. She realised that she'd need to create more avenues for connection to meet the deeper need.

When I'm working privately with a client, we use hypnosis to quickly reveal the subconscious beliefs at the core of the problem. Although I find hypnosis the fastest way, it certainly isn't the only way!

Techniques to Use at home to Reveal Your Subconscious Beliefs:

Meditation: Sit quietly somewhere you won't be disturbed. Spend a few minutes focusing on your breathing, relax your shoulders, and allow yourself to fully exhale. You can close your eyes or softly focus on the flames of a candle. Think of the behaviour you want to change. Close your eyes. Then, ask your subconscious mind, who or what has been driving this behaviour?

- What am I feeling?
- When have I felt like this before?
- What was happening in my life?
- What did I start to believe about myself?
- What did I start to believe about other people?
- What did I start to believe about life?

Journaling: When you're writing, I'd recommend a stream of consciousness approach where you write the first thing that comes to mind without questioning it or editing it. No one else needs to read your writing. This is completely private and just for you.

Start writing about the behaviour you'd like to change. Then, concentrate on the feelings that come up. Allow yourself to feel the feeling in your body.

How do you feel?

e.g., I feel frustrated because I try to speak up at work, and I'm not heard.

I feel___________ because ____________________________

Where do you feel it?

e.g., I feel it in my chest. It feels heavy.

I feel it______________________. It feels ________________

If this feeling had a colour, what colour would it be?

____

If this feeling had a texture, what texture would it be?

____

This feeling has a message for you.

Write: I'm the part of _____________ (your name) that feels frustrated. I have a message. I'm here because I want _________________ (your name) to know ____

These sets of questions are starting points and can be used interchangeably.

For centuries, our feelings have been short-changed. They've been delegated to the rank of second-class citizens beneath the status given to our rational, logical thoughts as if they are less meaningful, less valid, and less important.

Our feelings are important. It's essential to recognise them and process them. Our feelings can be likened to a GPS, an emotional satellite navigation system for life. Although I've always used the terms interchangeably, Brené Brown, author of *Atlas of the Heart*, makes an important distinction between feelings and emotions. She describes feelings as the physical sensations in the body and emotions as the labels we give to these feelings. This distinction makes sense to me, and I find myself using it with clients as much of my work involves a somatic approach, getting clients to tune into their bodies.

Emotions give us a shared vocabulary of meaning to use to describe our felt experiences. Research shows that our emotional intelligence is enhanced when we have a broader emotional vocabulary to draw from because when we can label our emotions more precisely, we feel better able to control our emotional response (David, 2016).

So often, when people are asked about their emotions, they respond with either "good" or "bad" or perhaps "happy," "sad," or "angry." This paints a very monochrome picture that doesn't do justice to our intricate emotional lives. For example, rather than just "angry," someone might be "livid," "annoyed," "furious," "peeved," "ropeable"… the list goes on, all providing more nuance to the situation.

When parents can model the use of language to describe their own emotions with children, they help to develop a child's emotional intelligence. For example, when a parent spills their coffee, they may say… "I'm really disappointed I spilt my coffee. I was really looking forward to a hot drink," or "Oh, I feel annoyed that I've spilt my coffee on this white shirt! Now I have to find something clean to wear to work."

It's important to be honest about the emotion because children can sense when we're hiding how we really feel.

Take a look at The Feel Wheel below. This may be a useful way to enhance your emotional vocabulary.

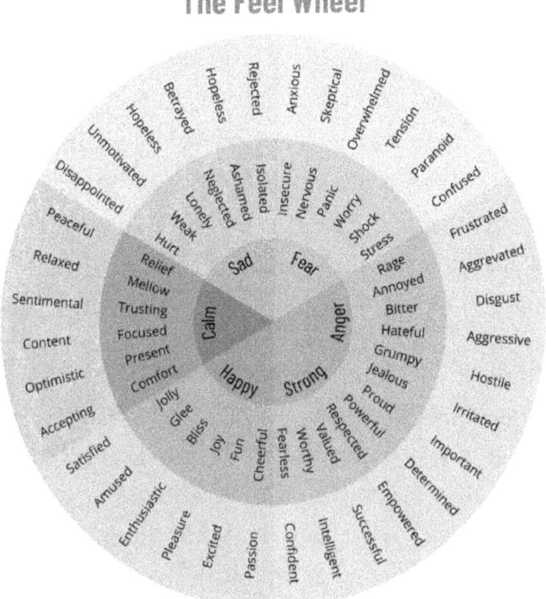

Writing Exercise:

Write three more words you could use to convey more nuanced emotions:

Joyful ________________________________

Sad ________________________________

Concerned ________________________________

Emotional eating is a big issue for many people. It can be especially challenging for three reasons. Firstly, no one can say, "Right, I've decided never to eat again, so emotional eating is no longer a problem!" Food is a biological need.

Secondly, we all have so much childhood conditioning around food and eating. Every family has their own way of doing things, whether it's sitting around the table sharing a meal or everyone eating on the run at different times.

When I was growing up, we were forced to eat everything on our plates and told that "There are children starving in China" so we couldn't waste anything. Also, my dad would want to watch the evening news while we ate, so we'd have to be quiet and would get in trouble for talking. Not the most relaxing way to do dinner! So, for me, learning to eat more intuitively and listen to my body has been life-changing.

Thirdly, eating and food are associated with so many celebrations and customs across cultures. Whether it's birthdays, weddings, holidays, religious celebrations, or simply going out for a meal with friends, eating is a part of the social tapestry of our lives and linked so much to what we do with others. Even meeting someone for a first date often involves sharing a meal.

What were mealtimes like for you when you were growing up?

Erin came to see me because she had an emotional eating issue, and although she wanted to drop a little excess weight, it wasn't really about weight loss. Erin already knew what worked for her. She felt good when she chose mainly gluten-free, dairy-free, lower-carb foods, and she loved to include some intermittent fasting in her weekly routine.

The issue was that, although she knew this worked for her, she just wasn't doing it. Erin was really going places in her career, and this now involved a lot of overnight travel. On top of that, she had a side hustle; an online venture that she was spending every spare minute on.

Erin gave me an example of what was happening. She'd arrived at her hotel and, as she was preparing for the conference the next day, she found herself ordering a cheese platter from room service. As Erin described herself doing this, she rubbed her hands together and laughed gleefully. She said it made her feel like a naughty little kid, doing something wrong and hoping they don't get caught!

During the session, we explored what was going on for Erin and what was subconsciously driving this behaviour. It turned out that a part of Erin was feeling bored and wanted more fun and excitement. As much as she loved her career and her side hustle, life had become all work and no play… and that wasn't fun at all. When Erin understood her deeper, internal motivation, she was able to meet the need for fun in other ways.

I guided her to access her inner wisdom, and she developed a powerful resource to deal with this urge for emotional eating. Erin's resource was a question to ask herself:

"What am I really hungry for?"

If emotional eating is something you find yourself compelled to do, you might like to borrow Erin's resource; pause and ask yourself the same question... "What am I really hungry for?"

Over time, you'll be able to differentiate between real hunger and the urge to eat emotionally. Real hunger starts slowly and increases over time. It's usually several hours since you've eaten. It isn't just for one specific food, and you may experience physical sensations such as a rumbling stomach or weakness. In contrast, a craving that's driven by emotion is usually for specific comfort foods such as chocolate, fatty foods, or salty foods and can occur even if you've just eaten, and there's often a feeling of being stressed, lonely, sad, angry, or bored.

I think most people exhibit a little of the Runner at times. If you find yourself doing this, the most important thing you can do is to sit with your emotions. Really tune into your body and feel your feelings. Listen to the messages. Know that all feelings are okay, even the uncomfortable ones. All feelings eventually pass, even if it feels like they'll be with you for eternity.

Jill Bolte Taylor, brain scientist and author of *My Stroke of Insight*, writes that when we experience an emotion as a response to something in our environment, there is a neurological process that takes place, and this process lasts for ninety seconds. This chemical response happens automatically, and we feel an emotion. The choice is ours if we choose to feed that emotion by falling into a negative thinking/feeling loop or if we allow the emotion to pass. I find it helpful to tell myself that I can handle the discomfort. I've done challenging things before (Hello? Childbirth!), and I can be present and experience this as well. I find it comforting knowing that it will pass.

It helps to be aware of your feelings.

Lean in. Really feel them. Label the emotion. Say it aloud. Breathe and release. Create some space and imagine that you're viewing someone else experiencing these emotions. Be the observer. What's the thought that's associated with this feeling? What is there to learn?

Of course, when we're grieving, that wave may be followed by another wave of intense emotion. We have to allow our feelings to flow. When they are allowed to flow, they pass. Tears can be particularly healing because they release oxytocin and endorphins, which can ease both physical and emotional pain, helping to explain why we can feel better after a good cry.

Mantras:

All feelings are welcome here. Even the uncomfortable ones—especially the uncomfortable ones.

I feel my feelings and allow them to flow, knowing they open the gate to new levels of wisdom, beauty, and joy.

I am not my feelings. I am not my thoughts. I am a divine being experiencing life.

I choose peace. I choose love. I choose joy.

Chapter 9

The Inner Critic

Have you met the Inner Critic?

I'm sure you have! You must recognise that inner critical voice that tells you in no uncertain terms that you've failed, you've made a mistake, you haven't made the grade. It's a harsh voice that always wants to take things one step further. Not only have you failed on this occasion, but it will also remind you of every other wrong move since you were five and then tell you that you **are** a failure… in some way deficient, stupid, worthless, and generally not good enough.

"Comparisonitis" starts early… and, initially, it's other people doing this on our behalf.

"How big was he when he was born?"

"When did she start to walk?"

"How old was she when she said her first word?"

I'm not arguing for zero awareness of a child's developmental milestones, as this can be an important indicator when there are delays and family members require additional knowledge, resources, and support. However, in the grand scheme of things, how important is the timing of these things really? When you watch a group of teens walking into school, can you pick who started walking at eight months old? Or who didn't let go of the furniture and take their first steps until they were 17 months old? Or who could read before they started school? Or who required a little additional support?

As children, we often hear adults compare us with our siblings:

"Oh, Rachael; she's the pretty one."

"Sean's got the brains."

"Colleen's got the height."

"Derrick has his father's temper."

And then there was school! Traditionally, schools have been established to educate to a set standard and measure children not just against the achievement of outcomes but against each other. Children are herded through the school gates like cattle and often have to follow a set path of achievements within a very cookie-cutter approach. This places so much pressure on students to perform and can lead to anxiety.

Singapore has long been regarded as a world leader in education. In 2018, the Singaporean Minister for Education declared that "Education is not a competition," announcing that students in both primary and high school would no longer be ranked according to exam results and there would be no examinations in Primary 1 and 2, among other ground-breaking changes. The change was a response to a study comparing Singaporean students to over 540,000 students from 72 other countries, and the report revealed that the anxiety level of Singaporean students was significantly higher than the Organisation for Economic Cooperation and Development average (OECD, 2017 as cited by Mae Echavez, 2018). The Singaporean education system now places greater emphasis on children developing social skills, self-awareness, and decision-making skills in response to a changing job market that requires different skills.

"Everyone is a genius. But if you judge a fish by its ability to climb a tree, it will live its whole life believing that it is stupid."
—Einstein

Do you compare yourself with others?

How does this make you feel?

Defeated? Superior? Ashamed? Inspired? Determined?

It's part of human nature to make comparisons. We compare two avocados and choose the one that's ripe to eat. We compare two cars and buy the one that best suits our needs. We can see a successful person in the same field, know that they're ahead of us, use them as a model of excellence and learn from them, or we can tell ourselves that they're just naturally gifted and spend hours critiquing our own shortcomings. This is the difference between healthy and unhealthy comparisons. Healthy comparison comes from a place of curiosity and openness to learn. We can see someone who's navigated the challenges of moving to a new country and say to ourselves, "If that's possible for them, it's possible for me." We can use other people's success as evidence of the good that is possible in life and have it inspire us. Ray Cummings wrote, "Comparison is the thief of joy." I think it's more accurate to say that "Unhealthy comparison is the thief of joy." In order for us to make comparisons in a healthy way, it's essential to manage our Inner Critic.

The Inner Critic can have a huge effect on our emotional wellbeing, and a by-product of this is reduced productivity. Delilah had enjoyed an extremely successful corporate career and, after receiving a large inheritance, had decided to give herself the precious gift of time. She took twelve months leave without pay, knowing that time is truly the only personal resource that is non-renewable. Delilah had always harboured a desire to become a novelist. She didn't share this with many people, but she decided that now was her time! She joined an online writer's group for inspiration and was paired with a buddy. The genre Delilah most loved to read was historical romance, so she began researching the colonial era set in both the United Kingdom and India. When she worked with me online, she was six months into her 12-month sabbatical and had only written 3,000 words of a planned 100,000-word novel. She had journals filled with notes and references, major themes, and plot ideas but very little actual writing.

When it came to actually working on the book as opposed to researching, she'd find herself procrastinating. Suddenly the pantry needed sorting right now, she felt compelled to visit an elderly aunt, and even the gym was more appealing. And when she did actually write something, she reread it every few paragraphs and started editing rather than allowing herself to experience a flow state and write unfiltered. When she reviewed what she'd written, she cringed… she didn't think any of it was good enough. Then, when she discussed her writing and progress with her online group, she saw that everyone else was far ahead of her in terms of word count, and she felt absolutely hopeless and then frozen…. the words stopped flowing altogether.

Delilah's Inner Critic was hard at work. When we explored what was going on subconsciously, there were several layers. Delilah had grown up with a mother who was very pushy and had extremely high expectations. Delilah's mother had been a gifted student but had fallen pregnant in her first year of university and had felt pressured to marry and concentrate on motherhood. This first pregnancy was followed by three more in quick succession, and her educational and career aspirations were long forgotten.

When Delilah was growing up, her mother took great pride in Delilah's educational achievements and later career success. Delilah's mother pushed her very hard to study, limited extracurricular activities, and was very harsh if she brought home a test result below 90%. She also constantly compared her to her siblings and friends. Delilah was already aware that this part of her upbringing was contributing to the problem. Delilah was a grown woman who was still working hard to earn her mother's approval. Her mother had been horrified at the idea of Delilah's twelve-month career break, and so Delilah was keen to prove herself with the completed novel.

The second layer was more surprising. When Delilah was in high school, she'd been a star of the debating team… words came easily to her. When she was 15 and representing the school in debating competitions, it was all on her shoulders to make the rebuttals and closing remarks. Usually, Delilah excelled with this pressure. However, on one occasion, a boy she really liked was watching. Suddenly, she felt very self-conscious and fumbled through until the end. Her team lost. She'd disappointed everyone and, to make matters worse, she was ridiculed for her ideas. Delilah developed a belief that it wasn't safe to share her ideas publicly and never participated in the debate team again. She felt herself pull away from certain friends and become more introverted.

When we looked at her life today, it became obvious… what can be more public than writing a book and having it printed and out in the world for anyone to publicly review? To Delilah, this was terrifying. What if people didn't like it? What if they criticised her? What if her friends thought less of her and pulled away? What if she looked like a fool? How could she cope with that possibility of shame and loss of connection?

Shame is such a powerful emotion. Brené Brown, social researcher and author of *I Thought It Was Just Me (But It Isn't)*, defines shame as "…the intensely painful feeling or experience of believing we are flawed and therefore unworthy of acceptance and belonging." It's a universal experience, and the fear it invokes can be paralysing. It can keep us stuck in loops of unhelpful thought patterns, fuelling an ongoing emotional response and triggering more thoughts of the same ilk.

Shame is two-pronged; on one level, there's the fear of inducing shame, and on the other level, there's the heavy shame we experience as a result of errors of judgement.

Most of my clients have been much harder on themselves than they would be on anyone else in the same situation. I've discovered clients punishing themselves for actions in childhood by holding on to false beliefs that they "don't deserve to be happy" and then sabotaging their own happiness. Justin was a prime example of this because, as a child, he'd been a typical little boy—active, adventurous, and inquisitive—but unfortunately, he'd been labelled as a "bad" kid and became the family scapegoat. If something went wrong, it was always Justin's fault. If his mum was unwell, Justin's father blamed him for making his mother "stressed." If he did anything mischievous at school, it was written in a book, which was sent home every week for his father to read and then punish him. This wasn't the teacher's idea; this was something his father insisted on. Justin's father was very strict and tried to control everyone in the family.

One day, Justin's mum suffered a stroke and passed away suddenly. Although Justin's father didn't say it aloud, Justin knew that the whole family blamed him, and as a 10-year-old, he truly believed that he was responsible for his mum's passing. It was only when he looked at the situation through an adult's eyes that he could see that the childhood belief was based on a lie. He wasn't a bad kid at all. Justin's shame dissolved, and he was able to move forward, knowing he deserved happiness just as much as anyone else.

An overactive Inner Critic can also lead to impostor syndrome. Impostor syndrome is "a psychological condition that is characterized by persistent doubt concerning one's abilities or accomplishments accompanied by the fear of being exposed as a fraud despite evidence of one's ongoing success" (*Merriam-Webster.com,* 2024).

Some of the brightest, most successful people struggle internally with this, yet to the world, they appear confident and accomplished. They have an inner dialogue that's mercilessly critical. If this resonates, it's important to know that you're not alone. Research shows that impostor syndrome can have devastating effects, often leading to increased levels of stress and burnout and contributing to a downturn in both job satisfaction and performance (Bravata et al., 2020). The effects over time are accumulative, so when you identify this pattern, it's easier to address it early.

How do we do this?

Firstly, remember that the Inner Critic, like all our Personas of Protection, is ultimately trying to help us and keep us safe. Instead of fighting with this voice, listen to it for a moment. Is the message accurate, exaggerated, or completely false?

Often, the Inner Critic only sees the negative, glass half-empty view.

Samuel was retired when he came to see me. He knew his life was essentially stress-free, yet he couldn't turn down the mind chatter, and his Inner Critic was a constant companion. This was even true when he was playing golf. It was supposed to be a social, fun activity, yet every week, he would go home and stew over the holes he'd missed to the point where he couldn't sleep! It may be understandable for a professional golfer to lose sleep over a game, but for a social golfer, Samuel knew this made no sense. He was reasonably proficient, and although about 80% of his shots were quite good, he could only focus on the 20%, which left room for improvement. Although he knew that this wasn't serving him, just knowing this wasn't enough. Samuel had to discover where this voice was coming from.

I invite you to pause for a moment and really tune into your Inner Critic. When you hear that voice, who does it sound like? Does it sound like one of your parents or a teacher? If you close your eyes, where do you hear the voice? Is it behind you? To the left or right? Or above you? Or in front of you? Many people realise that the voice isn't really even their own; it's often an authority figure from childhood.

The first step is to listen to the voice and thank it for trying to keep you safe. Now consider what you'd say to a friend in your situation. Would the voice be so harsh and judgemental? Try extending the compassion you'd show to a friend to yourself. Kristin Neff, researcher and author of *Self-Compassion: Stop Beating Yourself Up and Leave Insecurity Behind* asserts that the best way to overcome the habit of self-criticism is through self-compassion, self-acceptance, and treating ourselves with the "same goodwill we would share with someone we care about."

If there are any harsh words remaining, turn down the volume. You could even play with the tone of the voice. Would you pay as much attention if it sounded like a cartoon character? Perhaps imagine that it's Mickey Mouse or Donald Duck. You may even find yourself laughing. Imagine turning the volume down even lower with a remote control. Now, let that voice completely fade away.

Is it possible to silence the Inner Critic completely? One client asked me this, and I explained why I don't think this is possible or actually desirable. We need to have a part of us to evaluate our behaviour. We need our conscience to let us know when we're straying from our values and hurting other people or ourselves, and I think the Inner Critic reacts to this. The important thing for us is to listen to the message, evaluate it, apply self-compassion, and turn down the volume as outlined above.

The next step is to call on your Inner Coach.

What do they look like? Someone famous? A cartoon character? Someone you know?

What do they sound like? Sassy? Straight talking? Larger than life?

You get to choose!

Your Inner Coach believes in you and is there to encourage, uplift, and inspire you. Your Inner Coach guides you to step into your potential and try on new, empowering beliefs for size. This voice is positive and fills you with hope.

Our words, spoken and written, are immensely powerful. This universal truth has been passed down through the ages, from the Bible, "Death and life are in the power of the tongue…" (Proverbs 18:21) to "Raise your words, not your voice. It is rain that grows flowers, not thunder" (Rumi, 13th century Persian poet) to "Your words are so powerful and precious. Learn to harness them, guide them, and let them work for you," (Louise L. Hay, author of *You Can Heal Your Life*.)

We can choose what to say to ourselves and our loved ones. In coaching ourselves, we can use the first person saying, "I am strong. I am capable." We can also choose to use the third person; for example, I'd say, "Rebekah, you've got this! You're strong." When we coach ourselves using the third-person inner dialogue, it facilitates emotional regulation. Researchers suspect this is because it helps people to create psychological distance from their problems and view themselves in a similar way to how they see others (Moser et al., 2017).

Mantras:

I am worthy of compassion.

I am worthy of kindness.

I am worthy of love.

I am my own Inner Coach.

My words are powerful.

I speak my success into being.

Limitless.

Boundless.

Free.

Chapter 10

The Volcano

Have you met the Volcano?

The Volcano can appear seemingly calm and then explode without warning. Generally, the Volcano erupts with anger… yelling, slamming doors, swearing, storming off, but for some people, the pent up emotion is expressed as tears. Underneath the anger, there's usually a person who feels very hurt or frightened; perhaps their boundaries have been violated; perhaps their feelings have been hurt, or perhaps the world isn't working the way they'd like, and they're struggling to cope with the chasm between what currently is… and the way they think things should be.

Olivia came to see me filled with frustration, resentment, anger, and a very negative outlook on the world. She'd married Steve three years ago, after a string of bad relationships, and she was terrified of pushing him away with her behaviour. She'd find herself snapping at him needlessly, complaining endlessly about her work, and being generally irritable. This was also affecting their physical relationship as Steve had told her that sometimes he was too afraid to even sit next to her on the sofa and put his arm around her because she'd often push him away, saying she just wanted to be left alone. Steve had stopped initiating sexual intimacy and just waited for Olivia to come to him.

Olivia couldn't understand what was going on with her emotions. When she took the time to reflect on her life, she knew that she had so much to be thankful for… a loving husband, good friends, perfect health, financial success, and a career that could be stressful but was also stimulating and rewarding. She told me that she'd experienced these feelings for as long as she could remember. She'd tried mindfulness and counselling at times and improved a little, but nothing seemed to stick. She was filled with doubt about anything working and asked me what I thought was going on.

I shared this coffee cup analogy with her. It's attributed to Thich Nhat Hanh, a Buddhist monk.

Imagine this…You're walking in the office with your coffee, and someone bumps you, causing it to spill.

Why did you spill coffee?

You might say because someone bumped you, but this is only partially true….

You spilt coffee because that was in your cup. If you'd been drinking tea, tea would have spilt.

In the same way, when life bumps into you, whatever is inside will spill out.

If you're only just holding it together and wearing the mask of "I'm fine," it's easy to be triggered, and then whatever is below the surface bubbles up. Whether that's anger, resentment, fear, disappointment, or sadness, you can't hide it forever.

Yet, if we address the underlying subconscious programs, process, and release the emotions we've been carrying, we can ensure that our cups are filled with self-worth, compassion, resilience, and understanding. Then we don't need to fear being triggered or have someone bump into us… we trust ourselves to respond with grace rather than react impulsively.

The Volcano's subconscious programs are often linked to childhood events. If there's been trauma in childhood, it's beneficial to work through it supported by a therapist. Sometimes the trauma may be caused by a single event, for example, a home invasion or a parent's death. Other times it's multiple events over an extended period, such as growing up with an abusive parent, having parents who met a child's physical needs but failed to be there for them on an emotional level, or childhood bullying.

Human beings tend to continue doing what works, and any positive reinforcement of behaviour can be rewarding. We're not so different from Pavlov's dogs salivating at the sound of a bell because they associate the sound with being fed. They continued to salivate even when only being fed intermittently. If behaving like a Volcano and exploding emotionally serves to get us our own way, we'll continue doing it, even if it doesn't work every single time.

Some people start this behaviour in early childhood. I've had several clients talk about growing up with siblings who were emotionally volatile, and their parents found it easier to give in to the behaviour and ask the other child to "Just give it to them." To just do what they want because they'll make everyone miserable… reinforcing the behaviour and teaching the easier child that their feelings, needs, and desires don't matter as much.

I've had other clients talk about being known for having a temper as a child, and since they'd always reacted this way in family situations and been given their own way, they continued it as adults.

Sometimes the Volcano will say, "I can't help it. I've always been a passionate person."

We really need to question this truth. If someone is yelling and being verbally abusive, would they continue that behaviour if there was a knock at the door and one of their friends arrived? Or would they take a deep breath and hit pause?

The truth is that most adults can exercise control of an angry emotional response if and when they choose. Even when people are annoyed with their boss, seldom do they tell them what they can do with their job, especially if they have no other immediately available way to pay the rent. Similarly, if a police officer gives a directive, even if people don't like it, most will follow it, control their emotional response, and mutter silently in their head rather than getting arrested.

We all learn from past experiences and look for environmental cues to predict what's happening next. As human beings, we're meaning-making machines, and we're always trying to make sense of the world around us. If, as children, we grow up with someone who behaves as a Volcano, we may become hypervigilant, looking for signs that someone may be about to explode, so we can adjust our behaviour accordingly. If you grew up witnessing this behaviour, it can create a program in your subconscious mind that says, "This is what families do when there's conflict" and yelling is seen as normal.

Sometimes, anger gets a bad rap. It's seen as a negative emotion, and some people try to push it down, deny its existence, or blame it on others. I take the view that all emotions are welcome. Feelings are messengers, and they're in our bodies for a reason. Although all emotions may be appropriate at times, how we deal with them may not be. Some anger is, in fact, very healthy and necessary. It lets us know that a boundary has been violated and someone else's behaviour is not okay. Maintaining our inner peace hinges on what we choose to do with the message.

If we're feeling angry, it's essential to notice the feeling and hit pause. In practise with your children, this may look like taking a deep breath and internally counting to ten. During a heated discussion with your partner, it may look like saying, "I need some time out to process. Can we continue this later?" and walking away. In relationships, it can be a helpful practise to establish that either party can call a time-out during a discussion when necessary. In the workplace, during a meeting, it may look like saying, "That's a different perspective. I'm going to need some time to reflect on that and get back to you." It may look like writing a draft response to an email and leaving it a few hours or overnight prior to reviewing it and hitting send.

Viktor Frankl, an Austrian psychiatrist, Holocaust survivor, and author of *Man's Search for Meaning*, wrote that "Between stimulus and response there is a space. In that space is our power to choose our response. In our response lies our growth and our freedom."

We can choose to access this "space" in between stimulus and response consciously, for example, by focusing on our breath and extending the exhale or internally counting to ten. It's possible to do this and certainly better than exploding, but it can be challenging. It's far easier to access that space and choose our response after we've healed those core wounds because the emotional debris that we often hold on to after painful events has been released, therefore we're not as easily triggered,

Recent research shows that anger is the most difficult emotion to regulate, and although traditionally people have been encouraged to vent their anger to release it from their system, either verbally or physically, this is not the most effective strategy. When people go to a rage room and yell and smash plates, go for a run, or hit a punching bag, they are increasing the arousal of their autonomic nervous system, and this doesn't actually help to release anger. In fact, jogging can actually make it worse!

Studies show that decreasing the arousal through activities such as breathing, yoga, meditation, and mindfulness produces better results (Kjærvik & Bushman, 2024). Of course, everyone needs to experiment to find what works best for them. I've had clients who find that a 'runner's high' clears everything, so it really is very individual. I often find during a therapy session that the emotional release that comes with processing an event also shines a light on previously hidden subconscious beliefs. People finally understand why they do what they do, and those limiting subconscious beliefs that aren't even true are immediately shattered.

In the case of Olivia, she'd grown up with a very chaotic family dynamic. Olivia's parents had separated, and her father had left the family when she was only four, disappearing from her life. Olivia's mother used television as a crutch to help her cope with the challenges of work, loneliness, and being a single parent. Olivia felt neglected because, although her mother met her physical needs for food, clothing, education, and shelter, there was very limited interaction and emotional support. Olivia was an only child, and she felt her mother's anger on a daily basis. Olivia's mother was constantly yelling, pushing her away, and sending her to bed early so that she could watch television in peace. Olivia had carried anger because her mother moved after the split, preventing her from having a relationship with her father, and because she felt unwanted and unloved. Olivia was highly critical of herself, and a part of her felt unworthy. If her own mother didn't really seem to love her, who would? And could this love be trusted? These were the subconscious beliefs holding her back.

When we examine the interpersonal relationships of the Volcano, Karpman's drama triangle is often evident. Stephen B. Karpman, author of *A Game Free Life: The Definitive Book on the Drama Triangle and the Compassion Triangle*, proposed that there was a drama triangle at play in many dysfunctional relationships where people experienced conflict, repeated cycles, and appeared stuck, never able to adequately resolve an issue.

The drama triangle has three players: the Victim, the Persecutor, and the Rescuer. These roles aren't fixed and can be interchangeable depending on the circumstances.

In this dynamic, the victim isn't a person like a victim of a crime, but rather it's a role the person embodies as they claim to try everything to bring about change but are powerless to do so. The Victim has a poor me attitude and feels powerless, helpless, and hopeless.

The Persecutor is dominating and controlling, blames the victim for the problem, and reacts with anger, criticism, and finger-pointing.

The Rescuer appears and tries to protect the victim, alleviate their suffering, and solve the issue. The Rescuer needs to be needed and wants to save others. However, the issue is never resolved, and each participant may be having subconscious needs met through the continuation of the cycle.

Although the Volcano often takes on the role of the Persecutor, they can quickly switch to the Victim role and even the Rescuer role. Jack comes home from work and angrily berates his partner Ava because the house is a mess, and he thinks, as a stay-at-home mum, she's spending too much money. Jack criticises Ava, calls her lazy, and storms out of the house to meet up with his friends and start drinking. Ava feels helpless. She's had a challenging day caring for a sick child. She was up half the night, and now she's got to do the evening shift with the children alone, and she's exhausted.

Ava calls her best friend, Lauren, to explain what's happened. Lauren isn't surprised when Ava bursts into tears. It's a story she's heard many times before. Lauren insists on cancelling her

Friday night plans and coming over to help Ava, all the while thinking *Maybe now she'll go to counselling. Can't she see this can't go on forever?*

In this scenario, Ava is in the Victim role, Jack is the Persecutor, and Lauren is the Rescuer.

Lauren is still there when Jack comes home intoxicated at 11:00 p.m. She quickly leaves, and Ava goes to sleep in her daughter's room. The next morning, Ava is furious and criticises Jack for leaving her when the kids are sick and choosing alcohol over family. She steps into the Persecutor role. Jack gets defensive and moves into the Victim role, saying, "Nothing I do is ever good enough. You don't appreciate me working. I'm not wanted here," and he leaves. This cycle is repeated again and again… with the players never resolving the conflict if they continue to play these roles.

In my work, I've seen immense changes in relationships when a person who is presenting as a Volcano addresses the underlying subconscious drivers of their behaviour and is able to show up with more flexibility in their thinking and greater emotional maturity. When one person changes their behaviour, this changes the dynamic, and the other person often changes in response to this. For example, after Olivia did the inner work and healed the emotional wounding from her childhood, she changed her inner beliefs. She finally felt that she was innately loveable and no longer saw her mother's inability to demonstrate warmth and love as a reflection of her own lack of worth. Olivia released the hurt she'd been carrying around for years and found herself more at ease in mind and body. She was no longer reactive. She became a better listener and communicated more about her feelings rather than bottling everything up. This change produced a ripple effect, and her husband Steve felt emotionally safer in the relationship and became more affectionate and happier within the marriage.

The drama triangle can also be applied to workplace conflicts. Rita was new to her role in an engineering firm and was trying to find her place within the organisation. She was assigned to a group project and noted how quickly Paula pulled her aside to tell her how unfairly the work was distributed. Paula also claimed to never receive credit for her ideas and, as the only other woman on the team, she was looking to Rita for support. Paula confided that Dean, also on the team, was always trying to get in the limelight and take on leadership roles even though they were all on the same level.

Rita watched the interpersonal dynamics during their team meetings. It made sense to her what Paula was saying, so Rita spoke up at the next meeting, questioning how the tasks were distributed. In this scenario, Paula was the Victim, Rita was the Rescuer, and Dean was the Persecutor.

This continued at the next meeting, and then Dean was offended by some of Rita comments, placing himself in the Victim role, Rita in the Persecutor role, and then Paula spoke up to defend Rita and moved into the Rescuer role.

There are often subconscious motivations at play with these three roles. A person in the Victim role may have needs for validation and significance fulfilled by the Rescuer as well as alleviating a heavy burden of self–responsibility if they see the Persecutor as more powerful and doing something "to me." The Rescuer may have a subconscious drive to feel needed and may fear that their presence won't be wanted in the Victim's life if the Victim becomes more self-sufficient.

Take some time to examine your own life. Is there an area of conflict that you haven't been able to successfully resolve? Can you see yourself playing one of these roles? Do you ever play the role of Persecutor? Or perhaps the Victim? Or is there a scenario where you continually play the role of the Rescuer? If the answer is yes, it can be helpful to do some journaling about these questions.

Underneath anger, there is often sadness and sometimes fear. Perhaps a boundary has been crossed, taking away one's autonomy. Perhaps a deep wound has been inflicted, affecting one's sense of self and emotional well-being. Perhaps there is a significant threat present, and fear about a possible outcome engenders anger.

Sometimes, deep hurt results in a hardening of the heart, and the holding of anger blocks a person from experiencing peace and joy. After emotions have been processed, choosing to forgive can be a powerful way to let go of the past and move forward. When we choose to forgive someone who has wronged us, it's not really about the other person at all. The other person doesn't even need to know. It's all about us.

There is a Buddha quote that sums this up beautifully; "*Holding on to anger is like drinking poison and expecting the other person to die.*" Releasing the anger and choosing to forgive is something we do for ourselves.

An ancient Hawaiian practise supports the decision to forgive and let go: the Ho'oponopono forgiveness prayer. In *The Fifth Phrase,* Joe Vitale explains that "You're petitioning Divinity to unravel, release, clear, and remove that emotion. Ho'oponopono is used for emotional as well as physical ailments."

It consists of four simple phrases that can be used in any order:

I'm sorry.

Please forgive me.

Thank you.

I love you.

When we practise the Ho'oponopono prayer, we're seeking to release that which no longer serves us. We're asking the Divine to move us into a place of peace. The words aren't directed towards a person who wronged us, so if someone has deeply hurt us, we're not apologising to them or seeking their forgiveness; we're releasing the situation.

At its best, anger is a feeling that arises in the body with a concurrent thought; these are registered, the message decoded, and then it subsides because its job is done. Sometimes, the mind has a motivation for holding on to anger, believing that the anger will keep the story alive and prevent the person from making the same mistake again. If you're struggling to release anger, try this journaling exercise to dig deeper into the layers.

Journaling Exercise:

I feel____

I feel it in my __________________________________

I feel ____________ because______________________

And this is coming up ____________ and______________

It reminds me of___________________________________

And this feels____________________________________

Occasionally, I work with a client who has remained stagnant for many years in their healing process. They keep their eyes turned within, focusing on the emotional pain every day. They keep replaying scenarios years after they have occurred like a broken record in their minds. There is an energetic law: "What we focus on expands."

If we keep looking backwards, it's like looking at a wound and picking at the scab as it starts to form and then wondering why it isn't healing. A wise woman once told me that the windscreen of a car is so much bigger than the rear-view mirror for a reason; we're meant to be living in the moment and looking forward to the future we choose to create, not looking backwards.

Mantras:

It's safe for me to experience anger.

It's safe for me to listen to my anger.

It's safe for me to release my anger.

It's safe for me to forgive.

I forgive me.

Forgiving others is a gift I give myself.

I open the door of forgiveness and find peace.

Chapter 11

The Real Magic!

She exhaled, and everything changed.

Isabel walked through the door beaming, excited to tell me about yet another change. "My smartwatch has stopped beeping at me; it no longer needs to remind me to breathe!"

You may think this sounds like something small, but it was indicative of something far greater. Not only had we changed Isabel's inner beliefs and patterns of thought, we'd changed her physiology. Remember that your subconscious mind usually takes care of breathing without any conscious effort from you. Isabel's autonomic nervous system was being triggered by her inner thoughts and beliefs to engage the sympathetic nervous system in the "stress response," and consequently, Isabel was holding her breath even though, in reality, she was safe.

She'd started working with me, wracked with anxiety, constantly overthinking, and unable to speak up or delegate at work. Since she was in a managerial position, this was causing a huge issue as Isabel was doing all the tasks she was supposed to delegate. She felt sick whenever she needed to speak in a meeting. Isabel's leading Personas of Protection were the Overthinker and the Inner Critic.

When Isabel exhaled, she let go of all the old beliefs and felt internally at peace. This place of peace is so powerful because we can reset our nervous systems and wire in our new, empowering beliefs. This is where everything changes.

Physically Isabel slept better, breathed with ease, and even her chiropractor was amazed because her body was holding less muscular tension. Mentally and emotionally, she felt comfortable speaking up in meetings and delegating work, became more productive, and was able to support her team rather than doing their work for them. She started to enjoy work more, and this increased confidence and self-belief spilled over into her personal life as well.

Isabel had always been overwhelmed by the thought of online dating and had, in fact, avoided dating in general. She'd spent years concentrating on her career and told well-meaning family and friends that love would find her "when the time was right."

Now Isabel knew that a relationship was something she really wanted. She understood that Mr Right may not just appear on her doorstep without any action from her, so she decided to take action. She knew that it may not all be smooth sailing, but she felt resilient enough to handle rejections and hopeful enough to embrace the experience and make it fun.

Now it's your time to step up to the next level.

You understand which Personas of Protection have been standing in the way of you and success.

You've done the exercises to dig deeper into your subconscious programming, knowing that when we make the unconscious conscious, we can no longer blindly repeat the same patterns. Some beliefs shatter instantly because shining the light on them shows the falsehoods, and we can't continue blindly the same way. Other beliefs we recognise as unhelpful, we can actively question them and choose new beliefs, remembering that a belief is no more than a thought we've repeated time and time again until it's become automatic and unquestioned.

And hopefully, you've reached that precious place of internal peace and exhaled.

Now it's time to put all your learning together. I'm sure many of you are already familiar with some of the ideas and concepts in this book. If that's the case, that's a good thing because you've been consolidating what you know to be true and applying it to your life. Sometimes, I need to read things multiple times from many different sources for them to really sink in, and as I do, new levels of understanding emerge. This may be the same for you, but remember, knowledge is only the first step; applying this knowledge is running the race.

Acting on any of the ideas in this book is beneficial. All action moves the needle, but the real magic lies in putting it all together, like the layers of a pyramid built on a solid foundation, creating change that is both marvellous and awe-inspiring. You can expect others to notice this change, from a loved one asking what you're so happy about to a colleague congratulating you on a win at work and asking how you managed it.

Before I introduce you to the CREAM technique, take a moment to create a feeling of safety to help you do this work. Look for something of beauty in your immediate environment. It might be a plant, a painting, a candle… touch it… how does it feel? Study it in detail. What is it really like? Really look at it and smile… feeling the relaxation in your body and the good feelings generated within your heart. You can look at this object and use it to generate this feeling of safety if, at any stage, you become overwhelmed with the CREAM technique.

I named this the CREAM technique because I think of people as being like apple pie—fabulous as is, and perfect in their own way. Cream is what we can add to enhance the flavour.

I don't see people as being broken regardless of how they currently feel or the beliefs that are holding them back. No matter how terrible we feel, we're all only one feeling away from bliss at any time, and no matter how limiting our subconscious beliefs, we're only one aha moment away from adopting an empowering belief. Adding CREAM just makes life better. If this analogy doesn't resonate with you, feel free to swap the apple pie for cherry pie, or pavlova, or fruit salad. (If you're unfamiliar with pavlova—one of Australia's favourite desserts—be sure to Google it later.) Likewise, the cream could instead be ice cream, chocolate sauce, or gelato; the important point is that you're enhancing something that is already divine.

The CREAM Technique

Compassionate curiosity – what's going on? What are you feeling in your body? What thoughts?

Release – the stored emotions and unhelpful beliefs using techniques from this book.

Energy - raise your energetic, emotional vibration.

Align and Anchor – align with the new belief, set your intention, and Anchor your new beliefs in.

Movement – Repeat your mantra and move forward; first in your imagination and then by taking action.

Step 1: Compassionate Curiosity

Take some moments of quiet and cultivate compassionate curiosity.

Ask yourself, "What's going on?"

Tune in: What are you feeling in your body?

What are your initial thoughts?

Allow yourself to feel it, even if that means only touching the edge of the feeling and moving back out. Going into the feeling usually brings up additional thoughts and can uncover subconscious beliefs. We go through a process of feel… reveal… heal. Allowing ourselves to fully feel the feelings facilitates healing. We can do this gradually over time so that we don't overwhelm our nervous systems, and/or we can work through things with a therapist. This often speeds up the process.

Extend that compassionate curiosity towards others who may be involved in the situation. Try stepping back and considering the issue from their point of view. Does this change how we feel about the issue?

To maximise our emotional intelligence, or EQ, as it's called, we need to cultivate greater self-awareness, self-management, and social awareness. This process helps us to do just that.

Step 2: Release

Release the stored emotions and unhelpful subconscious beliefs. As you feel the feelings build up, stay present with them and then feel them release. Journal about the beliefs and feelings being exposed. See what else comes up that was hiding in the shadow below the surface.

Take your time with this process. Breathe through challenging emotions, taking your awareness back to the breath. If you start to become overwhelmed at any stage, return your focus to your "safety" object and then continue with the CREAM technique, either feeling into the feelings again or, if you've done enough of that stage today, just proceed with the next part.

Put your hands in front of you, imagining that you're holding the old emotions and limiting beliefs. Take a deep breath and blow them away. As they are blowing away, imagine them evaporating in a cloud of smoke. Do this three times, and then shake your hands and dust them off, releasing any energetic trace. Now you've reached a place of peace, breathe slowly and savour it for a few moments.

Step 3: Energy

Raise your energetic emotional vibration.

Own your energy!

Choose your emotion!

How do you want to feel?

I invite you to really think about this and consciously choose; after all, you've released the old, stuck emotions.

Susie Moore, life coach and best-selling author of *Let it be Easy*, claims that her superpower is being able to choose how she wants to feel. I love this! This is the type of superpower I choose, too. What about you? What is it that you'd like to feel? Close your eyes, put your hand on your heart, and lean into this feeling… breathe it in.

Need some help getting there? Where were you before you released all that old, stuck emotion? Which state do you want to tune into? If you're finding this tricky, it can really help to move your body. Stand up and do a full-body shake or perhaps some jumping jacks, or dance, or do a few yoga stretches. Play some music you love that generates good feelings.

Choose the emotion that would serve you now, close your eyes, and place your hand on your beautiful heart. Think of someone or something (maybe your pet) who loves you deeply. Feel that love, breathe it in, and then tune in to the emotion that you want to feel, breathe that in, and imagine the colour of that emotion filling your chest and expanding to fill your whole body.

Step 4 Align

Align your new beliefs with this emotional, energetic vibration. For example, if you released old, stored feelings of disappointment and shame and outdated beliefs about "not being good enough" or "the world is a tough place, and things never work out for me," then you might choose to feel joyful and confident.

What new beliefs would serve you? What about, "The world is my playground filled with new, exciting opportunities," or "I see new opportunities unfolding before my eyes," or "I've got this. I trust myself. I can do new things."

Choose a word or short phrase as your mantra. For example, "My time is now" or "I've got this!"

Next, set your intention. What do you actually want to call into your life? Choose a visual to act as an anchor so that whenever you see it, it serves as a reminder for you to tune into that energetic, emotional vibration and reinforce those new beliefs.

Your visual could be a picture from the internet that you choose to print or use as a screensaver. It could be a pebble you keep in your pocket, a piece of jewellery, or anything with the colour you love to wear. Perhaps even add a scent, such as an essential oil or perfume, and some uplifting music. It's your anchor, so it's up to you.

Step 5: Movement

This step is about taking action. Say your mantra and move forward, first in your imagination and then on the physical plane. Remember that your subconscious mind doesn't know the difference between what's real and what's vividly imagined. Use this knowledge to lay down the new neural pathways and reprogram your subconscious mind for success.

"*Imagination is everything. It is a preview of life's coming events.*"
—Albert Einstein.

Think of your intention, feel the feelings you've chosen as you raise your energetic vibration, and visualise yourself being successful. What would you be doing? How would that feel? What would you wear? Where would you be? Would you be alone, or is someone with you? Imagine this vividly.

Then, ask yourself, what's the smallest practical thing you can do today to move forward? You don't need to know all the steps. You don't have to have it all figured out. What's the tiniest step you can take? Say your mantra a few times, focus on your heart, feel your chosen emotion, and make that move today. Remember to congratulate yourself no matter how small the action.

Who knows? After you've done that tiny thing, your next move might be a huge leap.

You don't need to know all the steps before you start. You just need to set your intention, make a commitment to realising it, see and feel the end result, and take the first step. Keep a general path in mind and be ready to make adjustments. Aim to adopt a curious rather than a rigid approach so that you can embrace unexpected opportunities as they arise.

"*At the moment of commitment, the entire universe conspires to assist you.*"
—Johann Wolfgang von Goethe

Chapter 12

Plan for Success

When you first picked up this book, I'm sure you were curious about the *Personas of Protection* and wondered how they hold you back from reaching your potential and thriving in business and in life. You may have wondered about the link between your subconscious beliefs and your emotional intelligence. You may have even looked at the illustration that depicts the mind and heart working together, swinging on the trapeze, and wondered how it all tied together.

Thank you for taking the time to read this book and work through the exercises. Your future self also thanks you for investing the time and making these changes. I invite you to take a moment to reflect on how far you've come and congratulate yourself. Many readers start a book and stop partway through. You're one of the action-takers who follows through on their commitments, knowing that you signed the pledge. You've read through to the final chapter. Now it's time to create your plan for success.

Remember in Chapter 1, I outlined the 5 Ps—the promises of what you could expect from this book? Let's look at them again now.

Peace:

You've shone a light on many unhelpful subconscious beliefs and released some or all of the stuck emotions, allowing you to operate from a more peaceful baseline in your day-to-day life. This can be a process as new layers can be discovered as we grow and change. As long as our hearts are beating, there's room in our lives for learning! I find most of us reach a new level of awareness, consolidate this knowledge, and then make the next leap in a new cycle. I think a period of rest is vital, too, allowing us to "be" at this new level.

It's important to regularly check in with your body. If you feel overwhelmed and notice any physical tension, remember that it's good to stimulate the vagus nerve through your breath. You could slowly breathe in "peace" through your nose to the count of three and exhale "release" through your mouth to the count of six. Even just doing this a few times will start to engage your parasympathetic nervous system to move into the rest and digest mode.

If you notice any uncomfortable emotions, take a little time to experience the sensations and listen to the messages.

Choose times during the week to regularly move the energy within your body through activities such as meditation, breathing, laughing, and movement. If you feel stuck at any time, go back to the relevant parts of this book and work through the process of release and rewire.

Purpose:

I believe that even though there may be one overarching purpose to our lives, sometimes this may only be evident in part when we look back. Sometimes, we have a purpose for a season. In this work, I feel that I'm fulfilling my broad purpose of helping people believe in themselves to achieve success. I can look back and see that in my teaching roles, this was something I did well. As a child, I used to tell my youngest brother bedtime stories about Patrick the Great riding his horse through the woods and conquering all challenges. When I had very young children and focussed my time nurturing them, this was living my purpose. Working with clients is living my purpose, writing this book is living my purpose, and expanding my impact and teaching others how to do this is also living my purpose.

We discover our purpose by taking action. It can be helpful to reflect on what we enjoyed as children because often that holds a clue, but introspection won't always reveal the path. Getting out into the world, trying different things, and noticing the feedback we get is essential. Are we good at this? Does this light us up? It's trial and error.

One weekend, I had a beautiful exchange with the cashier when I bought my groceries. In this age of self-serve, I told her how much I appreciated her work. She explained how she loved connecting with customers, having a conversation, and brightening their day. She especially enjoyed her interactions with the elderly, knowing that for some of them, the connection created is an important part of the fabric of their lives. She further explained that when she was in high school, she chose not to go to sports but instead participated in a program where she visited the elderly in nursing homes and had a cup of tea and chatted with them, sometimes playing games.

She said she'd always wanted to do something working with the elderly, and she might look into it. Whether she ends up volunteering as a visitor or changing careers, she's very much living her purpose now through those interactions. Our purpose can be fulfilled in many ways; paid work is only one avenue.

Your purpose is about service. How can you make the world a better place? What problem can you solve? What impact can you have on an individual level? What impact can you have on a broader level? Living your purpose is saying "Yes" to life. "I'm here. I choose to play. The challenge is accepted." All the while knowing that there will be challenges, staying the distance because the cause is worthwhile. Living with purpose gives us energy and sparks joy.

Positivity:

When we embrace a more joyful, positive attitude, life feels easier, and we often notice more and more things going our way. Paulo Coelho, author of *The Alchemist*, says it like this: *"When you want something, all the universe conspires in helping you to achieve it."*

Have you ever noticed that happening? You're feeling good, things are going well, and more and more good things keep happening. I distinctly remember one such day. I was feeling excited because I'd just leased my first office for my business. I'd been shopping and found just the right cushions and accessories and seen my first client there, having a brilliant session. I left the office on a high and walked through a shopping centre where a young man approached me, just to wish me a happy day.

Chances are you've noticed the opposite of this, days that operate under Murphy's law and what could go wrong does. I wonder what would happen if you elevated your emotions, noticed what was going well, and actively looked for more evidence of this.

I love to program my mind to look for what's right. I actively choose input that could be inspirational… whether that's switching off the news and listening to or watching something I find uplifting or choosing to make time for creativity, laughter, and play. Notice beauty around you—from a ladybird to a sunrise. Some people like to have a favourite song or playlist at their fingertips which always helps them to choose joy. "Walking on Sunshine" by Katrina and the Waves works for me. I wonder what might work for you.

Remember the practise of gratitude we discussed in Chapter 4 about the Pauper? The quickest way to tune into the life energy of positivity is via the gratitude channel.

Performance:

When our Personas of Protection are holding us back, the internal conflict causes stress hormones to flood our bodies. Then our critical thinking abilities are undermined, our creativity switches off, and our performance suffers. Processing the underlying emotions and releasing the limiting subconscious beliefs is essential to getting us to that place of peace. We effectively release the handbrake and our performance skyrockets. Procrastination is a thing of the past because we're not impaired by the Inner Critic, the Overthinker, or the Mouse. We stop second-guessing ourselves, and that frees up our time and mental capacity to use towards our goals.

If you're having a particularly busy or challenging day and you'd like to pause and press reset to boost your performance, then I invite you to listen to this short recording. 'Take Time to Rest, Refresh and Focus,' is less than seven minutes and can be accessed here:

https://www.rebekahryan.com

Bob came to see me, fearing redundancy and desperate to lift his performance at work. At the end of his program, we had a frank conversation.

"I feel like..." Bob hesitated. "I can't say that."

"Go on, you can tell me," I replied.

"I feel like I could run naked down the beach, waving my arms in the air. I just feel so free, but I didn't want to give you that visual."

We both laughed. He came to see me burdened by the Overthinker and the Volcano, feeling stressed, constantly worrying, and highly reactive. He left feeling free, never happier, relaxed, closer to his wife, not reacting to other drivers on the road, much happier at work, and having more empathy for colleagues… and he told me all this before he even mentioned supercharging his performance.

Did Bob win the lotto?

No! But in terms of a life-changing result, it's arguably as good. It's the ripple effect in action. When you change the way you see the world, when you change those subconscious beliefs, you show up differently, and everything changes.

When it comes to measuring our performance, it's always beneficial to measure against our previous results rather than another person. Look at the outcome broadly in terms of result, effort, degree of improvement, how you felt during the experience, and what you learned for next time.

Profit:

How do you want to profit from doing this work?

What would be the most meaningful way to benefit?

I've worked with some professionals who want to free up time for their family by ditching the nine-to-five, working part-time in their regular roles, and starting a side hustle for some bonus money. Freedom and family are their highest priorities.

I've worked with other clients who have strong philanthropic values and desire an increased income to fulfil their purpose and start charities and not-for-profit organisations. They want to radically increase their wealth to do more good in the world. Some business owners want to create a legacy for their children, and this motivates them to expand and grow their income.

Candice came to me with a thriving business and a niggling idea that continually whispered to her… "Million dollar months, million dollar months." She'd been meditating on it and journaling, but the next step evaded her, so she decided to explore it during a session. Working together, we revealed the subconscious beliefs that were holding Candice back from this next level of success. She gained clarity on what it would take to more than double her monthly turnover, and she put a plan in motion.

This is all about being clear on your values and investing your precious time in moving closer to what you desire…be that travel, time at home with a baby, a new home, charity work, or an investment portfolio. You choose what profit means to you.

Intention

Are you ready to set your intention?

Close your eyes, inhale, and allow yourself the luxury of a long, slow exhale. Breathe in possibility. Dream big, and then dream bigger.

"Create the highest, grandest vision possible
for your life, because you become what you believe."
—Oprah Winfrey

If you momentarily question do I have what it takes or is this possible for me, understand that as we step into new arenas, new layers of subconscious beliefs can become relevant to our healing. As long as our hearts beat, we are feeling, thinking, and learning beings, and now you have the tools to support your expansion.

Setting an intention is a powerful process. It's essential to be really clear. Remember, you don't need to have all the specifics of the steps you'll take outlined because new opportunities, detours, or shortcuts may be revealed during the process; what you do need to be specific about is *what you actually want.* Be honest with yourself; too many people are so scared that their heart's desires aren't possible that they hold themselves back from even owning them.

Over the years, when I've asked clients what they want, I've noticed so many only speak in terms of what they don't want. For example, "I don't want to feel anxious in social situations" or "I don't want to keep holding myself back." If you struggle with this, flip the script and describe the opposite, for example,

"I want to feel comfortable and at ease in social situations," or "I want to step up at work into a leadership role."

"Every intention sets energy into motion,
whether you are aware of it or not."
—Henry David Thoreau

Be mindful of intentions, speak life into them and utilise that energy to your advantage.

Celebrate the Wins

There's something we can all learn from Christopher Columbus. When he was out at sea, he saw twigs in the water and recognised them as signs of land… signs to keep going.

When we're working towards a big goal, it can be easy to be discouraged. A voice in our head can say, *It's taking too long… maybe it won't work…*

At times like this, we need to put on our detective hats and actively look for signs of progress.

Write them down and keep the list somewhere visible. In a moment of overwhelm, it's easy to forget how powerful we truly are.

So celebrate those wins! Even in a small way. All too often, people dive headfirst into the next goal without even pausing to reflect on what they've achieved. When we do stop and celebrate, this releases a hit of dopamine—our reward chemical—and the more we do this, the more we'll want to do this. Then it's good to reconnect to your big "why." This ignites internal motivation for the next stage. Whether we're leading a team or self-employed and leading ourselves, taking time to notice our progress and celebrate helps us to go the distance.

Plan for Success

I'll know I've accessed Peace when____________________________

To maintain my Positivity, I'll________________________________

My Purpose is____

I'll measure my increased Performance in terms of ____________

I'll measure my Profit in terms of_____________________________

My Intention is____

I'll celebrate my wins by____________________________________

What next?

I'd love to hear your results overcoming self-sabotage and creating the success your desire, so please send me an email or tag me on social media and let me know.

I'm passionate about helping people overcome self-sabotage and boost their EQ to thrive in business and in life. If you'd like to explore working privately with me, please reach out via email at rebekah@rebekahryan.com or book straight into my online calendar via my website

www.rebekahryan.com

Are you interested in learning to do what I do? I've created 'SomaPsyche Insight' to teach my approach to hypnotherapists, coaches, and counsellors. Using these principles, I help even the most analytical clients to release their stuck emotions, update their subconscious beliefs, and connect with their own inner wisdom to thrive, achieving fast results.

Let me end this book sharing a little of Abraham Lincoln's wisdom,

"The best way to predict the future is to create it."

Bibliography

Ackerman, C. E. (2017). Benefits of gratitude: 28+ surprising research findings. *PositivePsychology.com*

Baumeister, R. F & Tierney, J. (2012). *Willpower: Rediscovering the greatest human strength.* Penguin Books.

Bravata, D. M., Watts, S. A., Keefer, A. L., Madhusudhan, D. K., Taylor, K. T., Clark, D. M., Nelson, R. S., Cokley, K. O., & Hagg, H. K. (2020). Prevalence, predictors, and treatment of impostor syndrome: A systematic review. *Journal of General Internal Medicine, 35*(4), 1252–1275.

Brown, B. (2007). *I thought it was just me (but it isn't): Making the journey from "What will people think?" to "I am enough."* Avery.

Brown, B. (2021). *Atlas of the heart: Mapping meaningful connection and the language of human experience*. Random House.

Coelho, P. (1995). *The Alchemist.* HarperCollins.

David, S. (2016). *Emotional agility: Get unstuck, embrace change, and thrive in work and life*. Avery.

Dictionary.com. Self-Sabotage. https://www.dictionary.com/browse/self-sabotage

Duckworth, A. (2016). *Grit: The power of passion and perseverance.* Scribner.

Duffield-Thomas, D. (2022). *Chill and prosper: The new way to grow your business, make millions, and change the world.* Hay House.

Emmons, R. A. & McCullough, M. E. (Eds.) (2004). *The psychology of gratitude.* Oxford University Press.

Forleo, M. (2020). *Everything is figureoutable!* Portfolio.

Frankl, V. (2006). *Man's search for meaning.* Beacon Press.

Goleman, D. (2012). *Emotional intelligence: Why it can matter more than IQ,* p.16, Bantam.

Hardy, D. (2012). *The compound effect: Jumpstart your income, your life, your success.* Vanguard Press.

Hay, L. L. (1984). *You can heal your life.* Hay House, LLC.

Karpman, S. B. (2014). *A game free life: The definitive book on the drama triangle and the compassion triangle.* Drama Triangle Publications.

Kjærvik, S. L. & Bushman, B. J. (2024). A meta-analytic review of anger management activities that increase or decrease arousal: What fuels or douses rage? *Clinical Psychology Review, 109.* https://doi.org/10.1016/j.cpr.2024.102414

LaFreniere, L. S., & Newman, M. G. (2020). Exposing worry's deceit: Percentage of untrue worries in generalized anxiety disorder treatment. *Behavior Therapy*, *51*(3), 413–423. https://doi.org/10.1016/j.beth.2019.07.003

Leaf, C. (2013). *Switch on your brain: The key to peak happiness, thinking, and health.* Baker Books.

Levine, P. A. (1997). *Waking the tiger: Healing trauma.* North Atlantic Books.

Lipton, B. H. (2016). *The biology of belief: Unleashing the power of consciousness, matter & miracles.* Hay House.

Mae Echavez, S. (2018). "Not a competition" Singapore removes class ranking system to encourage learning. *The Summit Express.* https://www.thesummitexpress.com/2018/10/singapore-removes-class-ranking-system-to-encourage-learning.html

McGonigal, K. (2016). *The upside of stress: Why stress is good for you, and how to get good at it.* Avery.

Merriam-Webster. (2024). Cognitive dissonance. In *Merriam-Webster.com* https://www.merriam-webster.com/dictionary/cognitive%20dissonance

Merriam-Webster. Impostor syndrome. In *Merriam-Webster.com* https://www.merriam-webster.com/dictionary/impostor%20syndrome

Moore, S. (2021). *Let it be easy: Simple ways to stop stressing & start living.* New World Library.

Moser, J. S., Dougherty, A., Mattson, W. I., Katz, B., Moran, T. P., Guevarra, D., Shablack, H., Ayduk, O., Jonides, J., Berman, M. G., & Kross, E. (2017). Third-person self-talk facilitates emotion regulation without engaging cognitive control: Converging evidence from ERP and fMRI. *Scientific Reports, 7*(1), 4519. https://doi.org/10.1038/s41598-017-04047-3

Neff, K. (2011). *Self-Compassion: Stop beating yourself up and leave insecurity behind.* William Morrow.

Rogers, C. R. (1995). *On becoming a person: A therapist's view of psychotherapy.* HarperOne.

Roster, C. A., Ferrari, J. R., & Jurkat, M. P. (2016). The dark side of home: Assessing possession 'clutter' on subjective well-being. *Journal of Environmental Psychology, 46*, 32–41. https://doi.org/10.1016/j.jenvp.2016.03.003

Sansone, R. A., & Sansone, L. A. (2010). Gratitude and well being: The benefits of appreciation. *Psychiatry*, *7*(11), 18–22.

Taylor, J. B. (2009). *My stroke of insight: A brain scientist's personal journey*. Penguin Books.

van der Kolk, B. (2015). *The body keeps the score: Brain, mind, and body in the healing of trauma.* Penguin Books.

Vitale, J. (2021). *The fifth phrase: The next Ho'oponopono and zero limits healing stage.* G&D Media.

Walker, P. (2013). *Complex PTSD: From surviving to thriving: A guide and map for recovering from childhood trauma.* CreateSpace.

Ware, B. (2019). *The top five regrets of the dying: A life transformed by the dearly departing.* Hay House.

Weinschenk, S. (2015). Shopping, dopamine, and anticipation: What monkeys have to teach us about shopping. Brain Wise, *Psychology Today.* https://www.psychologytoday.com/intl/blog/brain-wise/201510/shopping-dopamine-and-anticipation

Williamson, M. (1996). *A return to love: Reflections on the principles of "A course in miracles."* HarperOne.

Wiseman, R. (2003). *The luck factor: Change your luck and change your life.* Century.

About the Author

Rebekah Ryan is an award-winning clinical hypnotherapist, and relationship coach. Rebekah favours a holistic approach working with both the conscious and subconscious mind and the somatic wisdom of the body. Her work is a unique blend of logic, science, energetic practices, and spiritual principles.

Rebekah specialises in helping professionals and business owners overcome self-sabotaging habits of thought, feeling and behaviour, process their emotions and boost their EQ to thrive; creating happier relationships and professional success.

And in her own words…

Hello! Here are 10 fun facts about me:

- The promise of that first sip of black coffee helps me bounce out of bed in the morning.
- I'm mum to two gorgeous young adult sons, Lochie and Alex; and Ruby, a very spoilt Schnoodle.
- I live in Newcastle, a coastal Australian city, and work with clients all over the world.

- Music has always been a passion; whether I'm playing the piano, learning the ukulele or listening to the professionals…I find there's nothing better than a singalong!
- I love to bliss out with meditation and yin yoga.
- The ocean is my go-to place when I'm feeling emotional.
- I'm naturally very curious. When I was a little girl, I wanted to be just like Trixie Belden, the fictional girl detective, and was always on the lookout for a mystery.
- The power of the mind and expanding our potential has always fascinated me.
- I used to be a teacher before I was drawn to this work, and I believe it's never too late to find your "special" thing.
- Writing a book has been a long-held dream, so that's one more tick on the bucket list… visiting Italy might be next!

If you enjoyed this book, please leave me a review on Amazon. I'd love to hear your thoughts.

Contact details

Website: www.rebekahryan.com

Email: rebekah@rebekahryan.com

www.ingramcontent.com/pod-product-compliance
Lightning Source LLC
LaVergne TN
LVHW050649100826
845148LV00011B/2040